BEYOND ATTRACTION

Become a Man of Value Today

Vane Carnero

Beyond Attraction
Copyright © 2017 Vane Carnero
All rights reserved.

Copy Editing © Michelle Browne, Magpie Editing,
http://magpieediting.com

ISBN-13: 978-1544820125

ISBN-10: 1544820127

Stay hard !!!
V.C.

DEDICATION

To every guy who wants to know more about dating, and
wonders if this book is written about him.
Yes it is.

Also dedicated to my closest family and friends who
inspired me become who I am.
You are awesome.

Last, but not least, thank you Cacao Beach.
Thank you BG.

CONTENTS

VANE CARNERO

PART I

Introduction
to
HEAT Lifestyle

VANE CARNERO

CHAPTER 1

What Should You Expect From This Book?

My Promise to You

My personal goal is to bring some valuable knowledge and experience to the table, and let you have fun with it. I want to teach you how to be a true gentleman – both highly-respected and attractive to others.

How to Read This Book?

I would suggest you grab a coloured marker while reading this book and underline everything you like, or use the 'notes' and highlight function on your Kindle. Underline, make notes, put page marks on pages you like; do whatever will help you learn.

In few years from now, you will find the book in your library, open it, and guess what you will see then? You will see how much you have learned since the first day you opened it.

I've used this approach on all self-help books I read. I still open most of them from time to time to refresh my knowledge and to see how well I'm doing now. I learn something new each time.

Let's Be Honest

Remember, there are way too many people out there who will claim they are the best, and will turn you into an "attraction master". The secret really is that no one knows it ALL.

There is no one magical approach to dating that will make you a superstar. If someone is claiming otherwise, please, call them on their bullshit.

I'm sorry to tell you that, but I don't know it all either. I'm neither an attraction guru, nor a Master Pickup Artist, nor a Seduction Expert, nor Casanova himself reborn. I'm just a regular, normal guy who's learned a thing or two, and I want to share it with you. Maybe you will learn a few tricks, and maybe you'll find it life-changing, but this book definitely isn't the end-all and be-all of dating guides. Nobody's written that yet!

I am a candid guy who likes to keep it real. I haven't the slightest intention to tell you about things that I have not personally tried and succeeded at. Don't expect a "magic bullet" approach, but rather a creative combination of ways to get better at dating. For that reason, I have compiled a lot of what I have learned in my 20's in this book. It is all based on my personal experience.

I can tell you that awakening your inner gentleman by improving your dating approach will make you much more attractive and desirable.

Who is This Book For?

This book was written by a guy in his thirties for guys of all ages, based on my countless experiences in my twenties. This book is for you if you are someone who wants to learn:

✓ How to be a true gentleman in the 21st century.
✓ How to be confident without being needy, clingy, insecure, or creepy.
✓ How to improve conversation-starting skills.
✓ How to have a fantastic conversation, keeping it challenging and interesting, without breaking a sweat.
✓ How to have an exciting, dynamic and memorable lifestyle.
✓ More about dating in general, everything from how it works to what it means.
✓ Developing a personally attractive style, effective communication, confidence, and charisma.
✓ What to do if no one ever really showed you how dating works. The real deal.
✓ What to do when you might get friendzoned.
✓ How to feel confident enough to approach beautiful women.

The World is Full of Bad Advice

Have you noticed that not many people are experienced and knowledgeable about how dating works? When I started reading more on the topic, I found only ten to fifteen books on the subject. I had about five or ten friends or relatives at my disposal who were really good at it. This is pretty average, but it was not enough for me. Finding lifestyle improvement guides was even harder, nearly impossible.

How was I supposed to be become a true gentleman when there were so few people who could teach me the ropes? I'm lucky my uncle was, and still is, quite successful at understanding women. I picked up quite a few things from him.

But that's it. He was the only family member who could show me something accurate about it. Something real, not the regular nonsense and sometimes toxic ideas that people throw in your face. That stuff will just get you in trouble later on in life, and a lot of those ideas don't even work.

How many times have you gotten the wrong advice from other people about dating? Here is one example that's repeated all the time: Hey, go over there and buy that girl a drink!

Like most guys, I used to get bad advice all the time. People tend to believe they know it all. They tend to know, at best, a fifth of what they really should. Who knows how many of them can even explain what they do know? Maybe you've found that, too—about one in five of the things your friends may say will actually make sense and be good ideas! I certainly found that to be the case, and I hated it.

I hated lame, unsuccessful guys trying to give me lame, unsuccessful advice that got me nowhere. I had to learn it all by myself. To some extent, you'll have to do the same thing. However, you're not alone this time.

Set Your Goals, Define Your Expectations

Let's be honest. If you got this book, you probably have some specific questions as well as some general ones. One thing I've learned in life is that setting goals down will get you far. The next page is the perfect opportunity to put down your goals and expectations.

Grab a pen or pencil and put down your thoughts on a piece of paper, or use the space provided here for notes. Draw pictures if you are creative, draw a chart if you see things as a process, but don't overthink it. Imagine you have five minutes to act, and put down what you would want to learn about dating, lifestyle, adventure, girls, relationships, etc. Put down a date, a time, and sign it.

One day, you will open this book and you will see how much you have improved and changed over the years. Trust me on this one.

Let's get down to business. What do you expect to learn from this book?

_____
_____
_____
_____
_____
_____
_____
_____
_____
_____
_____
_____
_____
_____
_____
_____
_____
_____

Name and date:

A Few Final Words Before We Start

This book will guide you through the dating process. I will share my personal experiences with getting out of the friend zone, fighting the fear of approaching women, learning when to talk and when to listen, and much, much more.

As one of my favourite fitness coaches once told me, "I will show you what to eat and how to train, but I will not lift the weights for you." In the end, it is up to you to take the best of this book.

I believe you'll find out by yourself that I'm not interested in talking too much about one topic without going straight to the point I'm trying to communicate. Keeping it short and simple is what I like to do.

In all fairness, dating is not as complicated as we all think it is. Enjoying life is right at your fingertips. You probably already know a lot. It's just a matter of upgrading your skills, increasing your comfort zone, and learning how to be a true gentleman.

Have fun! Let's get on with the show.

CHAPTER 2

The Adventurer

Hello, this is your captain speaking. My name is Vane Carnero and it is my pleasure to take you through this journey that I call Beyond Attraction. I would like to introduce myself and tell you about my story. Please put your seatbelts on, fold your tray to the upright position, and get ready for takeoff.

I imagine you are asking yourself the following question, "So, who is this guy Vane Carnero? Why does he have such a strange name, and why did he write a book?" Here it is.

I grew up in Europe, and I moved to Canada when I was eighteen, just after high school. I spent my university years in North America. Then I moved back to Europe when I was twenty-five and a young business graduate, full of energy and desire to excel in life. At age of thirty, I moved back to Canada with my wife, and I am now fully enjoying my "family guy" life. I've lived in five cities, on two continents.

Lost you yet?

So, what does a married guy who emigrated three times at such a young age have to say about dating?

It's not my style to brag too much, but I had a lot of fun while dating in my twenties. I always looked at dating as a way to find my match, to find the woman that I could grow old with. Luckily for me, I was able to accomplish that!

On the other hand, it's my dating journey that you are interested in if you got this book. As you will learn from it I live to learn new things every day and to have tons of fun while doing it.

People tend to see me as a charismatic gentleman, but I tend to see myself just as an adventurer. My life has been a constant challenge, but somehow, I've managed to enjoy the most of it.

Like most guys out there, I also went through a period in my life where dating made no sense to me (at least not a complete sense). Did I even have enough self-confidence? I was good at few things, but I totally sucked at others. When I finally decided to tackle this battle, and I started learning by reading books, watching online presentations, and learning from friends who were better at me in the areas where I lacked skills.

I won't bore you with the details, but I was obviously dedicated. And even though it was not easy to learn these various skills, the results didn't take too long to appear. The actual and rapid success came through when I started developing my own style, with my own techniques and ideas, and my dating lifestyle got to the point where all those efforts paid off. Now, I am a happily married man, and I have the remarkably rare privilege of having found my "soulmate". We are a great team.

Hello, this is your captain speaking again. Sorry to interrupt, but we are approaching our final destination. Please put your seatbelts on and prepare for landing. In meantime, let's do a quick Q&A:

- ✓ Sports I have done? – Body-building, swimming, water polo, boxing, track and field, rock climbing, hiking, kayaking, kickboxing, grappling or wrestling, soccer, volleyball, basketball, and cycling.
- ✓ My favourite fruit? – Cherries; I love them. Bananas and berries are next on my list.
- ✓ Countries I have visited – England, Canada, USA, Cuba, Bulgaria, Romania, Greece, Mexico, Serbia, Croatia, Turkey, and Poland.
- ✓ Favourite car? – I love BMWs, but if money was not a factor, I'd drive a Hummer H1.
- ✓ What do I drink? – Mostly water, about 3 liters per day. But being raised in Europe, I do love beer, gin and tonic, rum and Coke, and of course whiskey and scotch. I love cigars, too.
- ✓ Day or night? – I admit it. I love the night, and the opportunities it brings. For some reason, I have more energy and my mind is much clearer at night. I like going out late, even for a walk.
- ✓ Pets? – I've had quite a few pets in my life – a dog, a cat, fish, frogs, turtles, tortoises, hedgehogs, tropical insects, newts, guinea pigs, parrots, hamsters... did I miss anything?
- ✓ My favourite TV Show? – Game of Thrones; oh yeah, winter is coming.
- ✓ Favourite season? – Summer. There is just so much more you can do while it is warm.
- ✓ My colour is? – Red, definitely red.

This is your captain speaking for a final time today. We have successfully landed. Thank you for being so patient while reading me brag about myself and how awesome and interesting this book will be to you.

It was pleasure to fly with you. Now get your ass out of my plane and go have fun!

CHAPTER 3

Confidence

"Inaction breeds doubt and fear. Action breeds confidence and courage. If you want to conquer fear, do not sit home and think about it. Go out and get busy." — Dale Carnegie

I strongly believe that having confidence will help you excel in every area of your life. One cannot overemphasize how important that is. Every one of us has insecurities, and every one of us at some point of time felt a lack of self confidence. We are human; it is normal for us to challenge reality by showing disbelief in our ability to cope with it.

What is confidence? To me, confidence is simply my ability to deal with life in a positive, respectful, calm, and controlled manner, while facing my fears with a great deal of self-knowledge.

We care about our family and friends, and deep inside, we

all want to be smart, wealthy, good-looking and happy. And to accomplish all that, you need to believe in yourself. In the following paragraphs, I would like to give you my own opinion of the topic of confidence.

Where does confidence come from?

There are so many books on the topic. The Internet is filled with articles on it. Some will say confidence comes from the outside world, based on our accomplishments, what we have, who we are, what we know. Other will preach that it comes from within, from our self-worth, from our love and contribution to others, from what we give.

I think confidence comes both from the inside and the outside world. Yes, confidence often goes up and down, no matter how well you understand it or manage it. I've noticed there are few particularly strong confidence boosters which can really have a magical effect. Check them out below. Think about which of them apply to you, or which of them you could improve on.

1. **Personal Accomplishments.** People who do sports, who are in business, who deal with competition on a daily basis, and are goal-oriented tend to be highly motivated by the results they accomplish. Their confidence goes through the roof every time they hit a target or accomplish a goal. It also goes down with failure.

Accomplishments are an external factor, so if you are motivated by them and happen to lose confidence, just remember one simple thing: every failure is part of a learning process. The moment you view it like this, failures can actually pump you up. Are you proud of your accomplishments? Do other people see them, or do they just recognise you as someone who enjoys accomplishing a lot? Focus on seeing failures as a step towards triumph, and see how your confidence rises with your results.

2. **Learning and Knowledge.** As I said in the previous point, some people get their confidence from their wisdom, their knowledge, their ability to learn new things. Those are the scholars of the world, the highly intelligent people, and the ones that can grasp concepts and understand complex theories. They might also be people who just know a skill, a trade, or have anything that produces value in their lives.

This is an internal factor. Knowledge is power, people say. I say knowledge is confidence. Can you teach others things you know? Do people see you as a wise person, who could provide accurate and unbiased counsel? Seek confidence in your knowledge and ability to learn.

3. **Looks, Style, and Appearance.** Not a big surprise. Some people feel great and have amazing confidence due to their physical attractiveness. Beauty is a great booster both for men and women, and is one of the most common external factors of self-confidence. Wonder why models or other good-looking people always look so confident? They know they are attractive, they know people want to be like them, and that pumps up their confidence level through the roof. The same applies to sexual energy, or what people call sex appeal. The sexier you are, the more confident you should appear.

You can always improve your appearance. That makes for an easy way to boost your self-esteem. Go to the mall, learn about styles of clothing, or join a gym. All that will make you more and more confident as you grow in this area.

4. **Social Skills and Belongingness.** Have you noticed how people who have a lot of friends, a wide network of connections, and are generally more social and friendly, are usually very, very confident? It comes from the fact that they love communication and interaction with other people. They get their energy from their internal belief that

they are popular, they have tons of friends, and that they will never be alone.

Are you considered a friendly, social person? Do you go out often, and do you like meeting new people? Consider increasing your social exposure if you want to get a little confidence boost.

5. **Money and Status.** That's a big one. Those who have mastered the financial game are usually some of the most confident people. They have all the resources to enjoy a lifestyle that all other people desire. They have a high social status, and they know they are few steps ahead of everyone else.

Not much more can be said here. Learn to make money and to spend it right. Strive for a higher social status. Even the process of chasing that goal will make you quite confident.

6. **Emotional Intelligence.** Yes, people who are in full control of their emotions, and can understand and control the emotions of others have not only great power, but also great self-esteem. This is completely an internal factor, and it comes from their ability to deal with emotions better than the rest of us.

Are you considered to be someone who has a great level of self-knowledge? Do you really know yourself that well? Consider reading a book or two on the topic of Emotional Intelligence. I still remember the first book I read on the topic. I was so pumped after I finished it, and I felt great about myself because I understood so much more.

7. **Success with Women.** If I have to look at the previous confidence boosters and choose the best one, this is it. This is it brother! Being adored by women, turning their heads when you walk by, and understanding how to be more attractive will make you the most confident man in the

world, or at least in your social circle. And the better you get at dating, the faster you'll unlock your inner gentleman. It will help you to be confident so that you don't need to come across as needy, clingy, insecure and creepy.

I once walked in a room full of people ten times richer than me, and I still had that calm confidence, so everyone noticed. I've personally gone to hundreds of parties with famous and popular people, and I still got noticed more than they do. I'm not the richest, the smartest, the most handsome, or the most social person out there, but I am a gentleman, and I know how to get women interested in me.

Confidence is a quality everyone admires. All good leaders have an abundance of it. They use their own self-esteem to motivate others, to inspire people, to get significant things done with ease.

The best part is that you see confident people every day, and even though they might not be popular world leaders, they still inspire you. Somehow you feel energised after you've met them. Their energy is contagious in a positive way.

Are we born with it, or do we learn it?

I've seen both. It's a quality some people seem to be born with, but anyone can learn it if they work at it consciously and hard.

With this book, I will try to touch on each of the confidence boosters, and how you could make them work in your favour. I will share successful tips to make you:
- ✓ Funny, but respectful
- ✓ Challenging, but candid
- ✓ Confident, but not arrogant
- ✓ Creative, but not weird

- ✓ Different, but not strange
- ✓ Chivalrous but not sleazy
- ✓ Persistent, but not needy
- ✓ Masculine, but not bigoted
- ✓ Adventurous, but not dangerous
- ✓ Polite, but not ass kissing
- ✓ Amusing, but not a clown
- ✓ Clever, but not condescending
- ✓ Attractive, but not self-obsessed

Often, very confident people are considered unconventional, following their own code and rules. I have noticed that in my confident friends, and I've tried to learn from them. The HEAT Lifestyle is my code.

My Advice After This Chapter

This book will guide you through the dating process, as I will share my personal experiences with getting out of the friend zone, fighting the fear of approaching, learning when to talk and when to listen, and much, much more. As you keep reading, you will learn more about developing an attractive style, effective communication, confidence, and charisma.

"I was fortunate enough to have an upbringing that made me more accepting of who I am." — Peter Dinklage

CHAPTER 4

HEAT Lifestyle

"Live as if you were to die tomorrow. Learn as if you were to live forever." — *Mahatma Gandhi*

HEAT Lifestyle represents a unique way of living that I developed throughout my life. I noticed that everyone dreams of living an "exciting life" but very few people actually accomplish it.

My main goal has always been TO LEARN MORE ABOUT HOW TO LIVE A PERFECT LIFE, WHILE HAVING A LOT OF FUN DOING SO.

Ready to learn more about it? The HEAT is on. To get the fire going, you need to be passionate, adventurous, motivated, ambitious, and completely goal-oriented.

There are four major areas of the HEAT Lifestyle – Health

and Fitness, Wealth and Career, Relationships and Dating, and Fun. The four areas are connected to such extent that if one suffers, it slowly affects the other three. Obtaining a POSITIVE BALANCE BETWEEN THE FOUR AREAS is your second major goal.

Now, let's look into those four areas in detail, using the specific rules I decided to follow.

Health and Fitness

Basics are simple. You want to stay in great physical shape for your age. People have to notice you when you walk in a room, and be automatically attracted to you because of your magnetic appearance. Here is how you can accomplish it.

Rule 1: I cannot emphasize how important sports are for your overall well-being. It keeps you disciplined, healthy, social, and makes you stand up above the crowd. It makes your confidence increase as you succeed. You should have at least one sport in your life; two or three are best. You don't have to play them forever, but take a shot at them. A healthy looking person tends to be more attractive, highly respected by others, and someone people often look up to.

Rule 2: Eating well is another area that you need to pay more attention to. When you are twenty, you can afford to eat whatever you want, but when you turn forty, it all comes back to you and slaps you straight in the face. Therefore, eating well is critical if you want to have a great lifestyle. I'd recommend you start learning about diet and nutrition as soon as possible. If you are already on that path, then keep going.

Wealth and Career

No money, no freedom. It is a rough reality. Some of us

choose to ignore and avoid it by saying "money is not everything". Have you heard it before? Yes, it is not everything, and money should not be a goal in your life. Money has to be a tool to accomplish your goals, not your master.

In order to get money, though, you will need to learn how to make it, how to control it, and how to make it work for you. I know from experience that this is no simple task to accomplish. Nevertheless, it is one that will bring you a lot of opportunities in your life.

Rule 1: Get a good, suitable education, and turn your school efforts into money. I don't need to overemphasize on this rule. Learning is a key. Being educated is something you will be proud of one day.

Rule 2: Learn to handle money well, both in moments of bounty and moments of austerity. For instance, I always use the simple accommodations rule I learned in school. It states that your expenses for your apartment or home should be one third of your income. It is a simple rule which always got me in control of my financial situation. Control your income and use it to give you freedom.

Rule 3: In order to have more money you have to be flexible and very, very ambitious. Go up that corporate ladder, and always have a Plan B. Learn to react quickly when you lose your main income source. Do not fear losing it; learn to accept it and move on fast. Most people are afraid of that and this way they become slaves to their jobs for life. This ain't healthy to both your confidence and your life.

Rule 4: Always have saved money so that you can survive in the worst possible scenarios. Until you save that money, you won't be free, believe me. I usually try to save as much money that will keep me going for six months if I lose my main source of income. I also learned it in school.

Rule 5: The last rule is to always have other options. Open your own business on the side, or get a second job, whatever helps you get that extra income, that extra security. This will give you even more freedom. Being able to drink water from two or three sources will always protect you from being thirsty.

Relationships and Dating

Friends, family and loved ones will make our life enriched and happy. But they can also make it quite miserable, so learn how to be socially successful.

Rule 1: Keep your friends close, and your adversaries closer. Learn to make friends with everyone; be the friendly, cool person everyone loves to be around. Most people, including me from time to time, focus on building strong relationships with their friends. That's perfect, but learning to have positive relationship with your enemies is critical to your success. Nice people will talk about you, but mean people will spread bad rumors about you, and try to put you down. Have a balance. Once you learn how to be a good friend, learn how to be a respected (or feared) adversary.

Rule 2: Family comes first, no matter how much they make your life miserable in some cases. They are your blood; your past and your future. Have a positive relationship with you family at all costs. Believe me, it helps a lot. Never neglect your responsibility as a brother, father, or a son.

Rule 3: Learn to not only understand the opposite sex, but to understand how you can interact better with them. A guy that is loved by all the girls in the group is called the alpha male. The same applies to a girl. You must learn not only how to attract, or how to seduce the opposite sex, but also how to keep them around.

When you are loved, you can excel in the other two areas faster than ever, so this area is the most important one. Learn to be a social KING, and people will feel more attracted to give you their affection.

Fun
You have to remember that there is a Fourth Area. It is called Fun. You have to obtain balance in your life while having this area fully satisfied. What's the point of living if we do not enjoy our lives?

Rule 1: Smile a lot. If you are one of these grumpy people, please stop reading this. Try to enjoy life in every way. Smile not only when you are happy, but also when you are not. Believe me. Smiling will get you farther than you'd think.

Rule 2: Travel. Visit new places, do new things. This enriches your life, and leaves you amazing memories. The memories are something only bad health can take away.

Rule 3: Celebrate every possible success. Reward yourself for being who you are and what you have accomplished. Holidays are time to let go of your responsibilities and just enjoy. Life is to be cherished; do not miss any opportunity to do so.

Now that you have seen all the areas of HEAT Lifestyle, is it time to think about the consequences of having such a dynamic and interesting life. The HEAT Lifestyle is fun, interesting, unique, adventurous way of living that makes your life richer in general. Nevertheless, there is one major pitfall – LACK OF PROPER SLEEP.

I love the energy that in the air, the drive, the adventure, but man, I don't seem to get enough sleep. During the week, I might go to work and do a sport.

Then at night, I would go out. I would go to bed at 1-2 a.m. and wake up at 8 a.m.

During the weekend, it is a disaster. I either travel, or part, or I do both. I go to bed at 4-5 a.m. and sleep until at least 12 p.m. If you manage to learn how to get better sleep, I would strongly recommend you do so. The HEAT Lifestyle is exhausting, but deeply rewarding process!

"No one is perfect, but someone has to try being it" – one of my favourite phrases. So be YOU. Be the ideal YOU. Give all you can, and enjoy every moment of it!

My Advice After This Chapter

Remember, HEAT Lifestyle is not just about being yourself, but about being yourself without neglecting your life and the balance between the four areas. Having tons of fun and a worthy lifestyle will leave something behind when you are gone.

Remember that we have one life, and we have to live it to our full potential. I love taking everything life throws my way, good or bad. Either way, I will learn something from it.

"To live is the rarest thing in the world. Most people exist, that is all." — Oscar Wilde

CHAPTER 5

Top 10 Mistakes Men Make When Dating

On my twenty-fifth birthday, I decided I had to do something exciting, to leave something behind. After all it has been a quarter of a century ever since I was born. I should have learned at least something by now. I already had significant experience both in the theoretical and the practical side of dating. Given the opportunity to be creative I wrote this article, as a summary of the most common mistakes men do when dating. Since I had plenty of experience doing them all, multiple times, I had to express my thought on a piece of paper.

We all go out on dates, but driven by our pre-programmed ideas of how the dating should work, we of often do one of the following mistakes. We mostly do them out lack of knowledge or experience.

10. Letting the fear of approaching stop you from meeting that one girl you liked. Have you been to a bar, or at a party, where you saw a girl you liked so much, but you never even talked to her? Then she ended up dating some other dude, very possibly an asshole type who was rude to you and other guys. This is a significant road block for most of the guys out there. Remember, you can make only one mistake on the way to dating success not having the balls to even start walking.

9. Falling for the phone/text communication. Ask yourself how many times you were in a situation where you called a girl, she did not answer, and you kept calling, texting, and leaving voicemail after voicemail. Then you got angry and acted like an asshole next time you saw her. I'm guilty of this one big time. But think about it; girls flake on themselves and the world in general, so why let yourself be affected by it? Understanding the phone/text communication should be your next learning goal.

8. Not paying attention to the girl's social circle and getting cockblocked. How many times has that sleazy BFF guy destroyed your chances of going out with a girl you liked? How many times have her girlfriends "saved" her from you? I personally got cockblocked so many times, it is not even funny. Remember, befriend her social circle first so they'll trust you. This is your first chance to prove you're not a weirdo, creep, or a predator!

7. Going into the friend zone. I know you guys expected this one. You attract the girl, you build comfort, but you just don't seem to be able to go any further. Then she starts dating some guy with tattoos, or whatever else you end up irrationally hating—maybe he drives a big truck, maybe he has a stupid job, you name it. The friend zone is a place you never want to end up in. Nevertheless, it happens to all of us.

6. Lacking smoothness in your dating approach. This was my most common mistake. You rush things, you want to get to the end faster and you skip important steps, you go for the kiss before establishing enough comfort, or you are not diplomatic and tactful enough. Then the girl refuses to even talk to you, she gets scared, and she starts dating that bum BFF just because she feels more comfortable around him, and because your failure is other people's success. Don't you hate that? Make sure you finish on a high note after every interaction, and take it step by step.

5. Not moving forward when you had a chance. Man, this happened when we were young almost all the time. There was this cute girl that was obviously in love with you, but you were in love with some girl (because all the other guys liked her, so you fell for her too). So you didn't pay attention to the girl that liked you and kept chasing the one that others liked. Then you lost them both. In the end, it was you and your hand.

4. Having a wrong idea about how a man should act. "I'm a smart guy, you know? I'm not like those assholes that cheat on their girlfriends, I do not date other women; I buy her presents, I take her out, and I show her tons of interest. I'm so different than the rest. I'm a nice guy". Admit it, you've had that though in your head at least once in your life. Guess what? Don't mistake being a great guy for being a nice guy.

3. Not paying enough attention and importance to the dating process and the way it can change your life. You have exams, you have to work, you have no cash, your time is limited; excuses, excuses, excuses. You can't learn how to be a good guitar player unless you keep learning and keep practicing. How do you expect to be a good at dating when you constantly find reasons not to do it often? Been there, made that mistake.

2. Getting emotional, letting those feelings control you, becoming needy, losing yourself slowly and painfully, or what we call Lust Sickness. Lust Sickness at its late or early stages is a reason for over 80% of our mistakes. This mistake can lead you to all the other mistakes listed above. You get angry quickly, you lose it, and break up with her because you feel she'll break up with you first. You start arguing with her, acting like you don't care or being a caveman for no particular reason, only wanting sex and nothing else, etc. We are all guilty of this chronic disease, as it is in our genes. Try not to let it out.

What do you think is the number one mistake? I'll give you a hint. It leads to all the other mistakes that can cause Love Sickness to burst out. If you don't fix it on time, it will damage not only your dating life, but also everything else. You probably guessed it right.

1. Lack of Confidence. I think there is no need for further explanation. NO BALLS, NO DATES. Having an interesting life and believing in yourself will give you an edge in your dating…it will give you huge advantage to be realistic. Know who you are and what you can offer, if you somehow you feel you can't offer much, go out there and learn a few things to raise your value – salsa, guitar, magic, psychology, any type of sport, etc.

My Advice After This Chapter

Let's take a minute to think about those mistakes and laugh for a bit. This book will hopefully help you with the mistakes above. It is designed from my personal experience to assist you in your journey and help you avoid some of them. You are already reading it, so you are on the right path.

I always enjoyed being a gentleman above all!

Heads up! Our genes and our upbringing can affect who we are, but cannot affect who we become! Remember it every day!

"If you live long enough, you'll make mistakes. But if you learn from them, you'll be a better person. It's how you handle adversity, not how it affects you. The main thing is never quit, never quit, never quit."
— *Bill Clinton*

VANE CARNERO

CHAPTER 6

Please Don't Go Out and Start Approaching Random Women on the Streets!

What are the commonalities between cold-calling jobs, door-to-door advertising, and approaching random women on the streets? It tells people, you are not capable of getting a decent job, or you have no connections and friends. It tells people you are a needy person with no other options. And how would you respect yourself if that is the perception you leave?

I will also admit it. I did few of those cold-calling jobs myself. Many of my friends did it too. None of us stayed there, because it made us feel creepy, needy, and desperate. I know from experience how lame it is.

It is the same with cold approaching random women on the streets, absolutely the same!

I do understand many people out there will tell you that in order to defeat your fear of approaching women you will have to start by randomly approaching people on the streets. Those people will try to sell you the concepts of "practice makes perfect", "follow this script", "do as I tell you", etc. So they will take you out downtown, give you a script, and ask you to approach as many women as you can. How disrespectful to women is that?

But you are smarter than that. You are not a script reader. You want to be able to create your out reality, not to invade someone else's. You want to be respected.

Ask any girl if she likes random guys approaching her on the streets. Please do, and see what the answer is.

Why do I think the random cold approach is LAME?

- ✓ Doesn't actually come from connection of any kind
- ✓ Shows neediness and desperation
- ✓ Is disrespectful and uninvited
- ✓ Can get you in trouble with law enforcement
- ✓ Gives you a bad image
- ✓ Has a very low success rate

It also puts an invisible label on your forehead which reads, "Too pushy, weird, arrogant, disrespectful, sleazy, needy, dangerous, clownish, condescending, and self-obsessed!"

My Advice After This Chapter

This is the main reason the pickup community has such a bad reputation. It is because of the thousands of zombies crawling downtown at lunch time trying to "pick up" women, because someone else told them to do so. I honestly believe people like this should be arrested.

Don't fall for it. Do it right. There is no magic pill, there are no shortcuts. There is you, your confidence, your interesting personality, and you knowledge. Creeping out random people on the streets is neither classy, nor a source for pride.

VANE CARNERO

PART II

Get the Basics Straight and Unlock the Secrets of Gentleman's Code

VANE CARNERO

CHAPTER 7

Don't Be That Guy!

Is there a better way to start talking about the basics of dating then to ask a girl for her opinion on the matter? This chapter is written by my lovely wife Denny, and it will show you what a girl dislikes in a guy. I already had my share on the topic in the "Top 10 Mistakes" chapter, but I'm happy she agreed to put down few words on the topic. It's always beneficial to get a woman's perspective on dating. Enjoy!

Types of Guys Women Avoid Dating by Denny

As you expand your dating life, you subconsciously (or consciously) realize what types of women you do not want to date – the drama queen, the gold-digger, the psycho girl, etc. Everybody has their own type they never want to date again, right? The point is to never stop looking. There is no right formula or a template that you should be using, so be your own hero.

But just as men are attracted to certain types of women, there are types of men that women avoid. And trust me, I am speaking from experience. Sometimes ten-minute conversation or less is enough for a woman to never want to see you again. The solution is not to entirely change your personality, but to open up your mind, to emotionally educate yourself, and to try to see the world from different angles.

Until then, let me present you five types of men women avoid dating. Please don't be that guy. Just... don't.

1. The Workaholic

Every woman wants the man she is dating to have a job, to be successful, to be able to afford going out with her (do not mistake this for meaning "to pay her bills" if you are talking about a cool chick), to be financially independent, and to be responsible. But imagine being a woman going on a date with a guy obsessed with his job, whose life is all about work, his coworkers, and the next report he is about to submit. Yes, he would probably be a great companion when discussing growing in a company, the latest sales pitch he'd heard of, auditing trends, or marketing strategies, depending on the field he works in.

Or my favourite: the latest Microsoft Excel function which allows you to filter and calculate data with MAXIFS and MINIFS. How cool is that?! How about constantly talking about his co-worker Adam who is also his best (and only) friend, and how they made the best product presentation ever. Imagine a detailed presentation with dollar amounts, margin numbers, and a three-month profit forecast.

Honestly, that is great only if you are still at work and celebrating a successful day with coworkers - the people you are used to spending 40 hours a week anyway.

I am NOT saying not to talk about work.

Work is a huge part of our life, but not our whole life. Learn to enjoy life in every aspect. And by the way, your date probably goes to work, too (not necessarily but quite possible). Sharing what you do at work can be great, especially when you love what you do. If you are lucky enough to love your job, show how passionate you are about it, but don't forget to let your date talk and ask you questions.

Funny situations happen at the office every day, and those are definitely worth sharing. And by funny, I mean goofy, silly, ridiculous…see where I am going? Focus on human angles, as reporters call them.

2. Mr. Know-It-All

Confidence is sexy, that's for sure. Being able to discuss different topics and share an adequate opinion on them definitely gives you credit. But if you have a huge ego, do not know when to shut up and let the other person talk, and have the desire to always be right, you are either a ten-year-old, or extremely insecure. Sorry, but either way, you lose.

Mr. Know-It-All is often very judgemental, too. He has experienced everything life can offer (that's what he's said, right?) and is ready to turn every conversation into an argument just because he thinks he knows better. Biggest turn-off ever. This is also the point where most women start acting defensively. Did you take a woman on a date to get to know her, or what?! The purpose of a date is to relax and to have fun. There is no fun in having to argue with someone you barely know.

Remember that a girl's attention for your story is limited, and unfortunately for you, you only have a few minutes before she starts making assumptions. So be interesting, be a gentleman, be a storyteller, ask questions and listen.

Your stories may be awesome, but going on a date is not a one-man show. Know when to stop talking about yourself and learn to lead a conversation by asking the right questions at the right moment. Follow her story and show respect.

3. Mama's Boy

It's great for a person to be close to their parents! Being in a good relationship with your mom and/or dad gives you the feeling you are always supported and loved. However, being too attached to your parents in your late twenties is kind of weird, don't you think?

If you are a guy that cannot make a decision without calling his mom, and you still need her approval to do anything, you are not looking for a woman. You are looking for a second mother. You probably like to be told what to do because you want to avoid making a mistake, or because you are too lazy to take responsibility for anything.

Do you even realize what kind of woman you would attract in your life if you are this guy? A control freak would be very cute to name it. And let's not mention how much she and your mother would hate each other. Even though, if you are lucky enough, your mom would probably be happy she doesn't have to worry about her baby boy anymore. Who knows?

Bad news: an attractive, interesting and smart woman would never date you. Even if she makes the mistake of going out with you once, she might leave while you are one the phone with your mom for the third time for the last hour.

Good news: you can fix this. Stop seeking out your parents' approval to enjoy life. Don't be afraid to make a mistake. Be the grown-up man you already are and take responsibility when things go wrong. Meet new people. Go on an adventure. You will soon realize that you need your parents for new reasons: to share interesting life stories with, to brainstorm important life decisions and that also they might need your support and love more than you need theirs.

4. The Needy One

The needy guy is the complete opposite of Mr. Know-It-All, and very often a Mama's boy – too sensitive, emotionally uncontrolled, and socially awkward. The law of attraction does exist. Women are attracted to men's confidence, strength and independence. If there is anything a man should not be, it's needy and desperate. And trust me, desperation reeks from a guy.

You might also be the sweetest guy ever, you might look confident and laid back at first, but if you keep messaging her constantly without giving her a chance to message you back, to show some interest in you, especially if she keeps avoiding your messages, you start to look creepy. Don't take her attention or your own specialness for granted!

You might want her a lot more than she wants you, and you've assumed it's mutual because you're so desperate for company. And creepy is the last thing you want a woman to think you are.

But let's assume she gave you a chance, or was just trying to be polite and answered your messages once in a while.

You are probably the fifth guy on the line that she does that to.

The reason for this is very simple. You are there to boost her confidence, she wants to feel wanted, but has no intention of wanting you back. And guess what? You are definitely in the friend zone already, a person whose company is tolerable or sometimes fun, but not someone she feels chemistry with. The moment she gets the guy she wants, you will be forgotten, and considering you are desperately in love with who you think she is, you will be heart-broken.

5. Mr. Bad (or No) Manners

This one actually applies to everyone – whether a man or a woman. It's not a pleasant topic to talk about, but it definitely needs some attention. Nobody is perfect, we know that, and we all have habits that annoy other people.

But having even just one of the listed below would probably make your date consider abandoning the ship:

✓ **Poor hygiene** – I am putting this one first just because I want to finish with it and never come back to discussing it, ever. Don't go to a date if you're stinky, without taking shower prior the date, with bad breath, smelling like a wet dog, or wearing dirty clothes. I have always thought this is common sense. Unfortunately, that is not correct.

✓ **Talking with your mouth full OR chewing with your mouth open.** Ew! We all saw what your steak looked like in your plate; no need to see it being digested.

✓ **Being rude to the waiter/waitress** – what would you think of a person that is super nice to you, keeps smiling at you, laughs with you, and then a second later is mean, condescending, and rude to the waiter/waitress? If THAT is not a two-faced bitch, I don't know who is.

✓ **Interrupting** – be a gentleman, okay? If you like hearing your own voice that much, you should probably lead a one-man show or simply go out with your friends that will tell you're an asshole and ignore you anyway.

✓ **Smartphones** – it's the twenty-first century, we get that. But updating your apps, texting your best friend, talking on the phone, taking pictures of your meal for Instagram, or posting stuff on Facebook while on a date can wait. It is disrespectful, even if the woman you date is boring.

Relationships and dating are complex matters, but you can always find joy in learning new things every day. Try to be the best "you", and watch out for your own bad habits. Good Luck!

My Advice After This Chapter

I should go thank Denny for the great chapter she wrote. I laughed so hard when I first read it, because I have encountered all of these guys on a daily basis. Yep, I still meet a lot of people who act like that.

And if I think about it, I'm also guilty of acting like almost all of them at some point in my life (never been a mama's boy). You will read more about my point of view and the errors I made in the following chapter. You will also learn about improving your behaviour by seeing things from other people's point of view.

I guess the major point here is to try and see yourself in the mirror. Think about your actions. Are they demanding, are they rude, are they annoying? Are you mistaking being a stalker for being persistent? Are you way too dependent on other people? If the answer is yes, then try to avoid doing what you do and learn the right approach. This book is intended to help you do exactly that.

Last but not least, start talking to more women in general, not only for dating purposes. Learn what they like and what they don't. Being around women will also make you treat them more normally so that you don't lose your cool or turn into a gibbering idiot when you spend time around a woman, any woman.

CHAPTER 8

The Point of View

"Strength does not come from winning. Your struggles develop your strengths. When you go through hardships and decide not to surrender, that is strength." — *Arnold Schwarzenegger*

When it comes to dating, the point of view is extremely important and critical for the final outcome. Here I'll share some thoughts that I have on this topic and I'll discuss my own approach. I hope that topic can get you thinking.

First, I was that dude, like every teenager at fourteen or fifteen, who just wants to date beautiful women. My first approach was "get drunk, have fun". Growing up in Europe at that time also gave me great access to clubbing experiences. Yes, back then, we went out and dancing. Not anymore. It worked well, but something was missing and I was not succeeding the way I wanted. My confidence was just not there yet.

So I shifted to being the nice guy. Here was my first major mistake, but hey, you gotta go through this stage. And so I did. I tried to "act nice, be a gentleman, respect women, do anything to get girls' attention." I did succeed with this approach as well, but again, something was missing. Girls felt attraction for me, but I barely managed to go any further. If I managed to get a girlfriend, it was mostly due to charm and luck, not a focused decision.

Then after few significant failures, I got angry, really angry at girls, and I adopted a bad boy point of view – "do as you please, and care only about yourself." Here, I got a lot of success, tons of it, actually. Somehow it frickin' worked. But nevertheless, I managed to hurt a lot of people, and lost many friends. I felt a need to shift again.

Then I adopted the adaptation strategy. I was trying to figure out what women want and use the appropriate strategy. Instead of being one guy, I was shifting my personality at will. It worked too, but it was a hit and miss philosophy. Why? I didn't know how to select the right approach.

Man, women were acting differently each time. I was unable to really figure out what they wanted.

At last, I read few classic books on the topic of dating and my life changed for good. The first thing I learned was that women see men as either lovers or providers. If you are considered as a lover, then they'll have sex with you; however, if you are considered a provider they'll like the safety you give them, but withhold sex.

It's worth researching the topic, as this theory originates from Charles Darwin, and his laws of Evolution and Attraction. Darwin's ideas of evolution actually come from the idea of being fittest to one's environment, as that's how creatures survive. They meet the needs of other individuals in their species and can adapt to changing pressures. Just memorizing something won't do the trick, but what the HEAT lifestyle offers is a variety of techniques to keep guys adapting and being the best version of themselves.

After learning all that from all the books I'd read and all the practice I had, there was another shift in thinking for me. I became the lover. I started expressing my attractive personality, focused more on being interesting in a unique way, and they all liked it. I became quite desired young man in my twenties. I started enjoying life much more as I managed to drop down all of my limiting beliefs.

I have seen many guys go through that change, and they doubled their dating, and some of them even met their future wives. How cool is that? In order to evolve, you need to go to the basics. Being adaptable to change, accepting responsibility for your own development, learning new things every day, and being flexible is something, which will help you develop emotionally as an adult. In this book, I will show you how you can achieve it.

So, the whole purpose of that LOOOOOOOONG story was that your point of view is crucial to your dating success. I have figured something out that works, a point of view that can improve your success without having to go over all the stages I mentioned above. Keep reading and get on the fast track!

The Good, the Bad, and the Ugly

Now, let's go back to my twenties. During that time, I hit a point in my life where dating was quite important to my well-being. In fact, most of us out there hit that same point. Now, I have a clear view of the dating lifestyle and how it works. Some call it "the game", others, "pickup artistry". I like to call it just dating.

I'm at a point where I know when I messed up. A decent self-assessment is something for which we should all strive. I also know where other people have messed up based on what they tell me about their game plan.

Let's look at some simple formulas which will help you understand the dating process much better. Here is my breakdown of how things work, giving you the most basic and short analysis I can think of (without spending twenty million pages on it, of course).

Excellent Dating = good health, good friends, becoming an alpha male, lots of sex, lots of attention, lots of respect, better social skills, and many, many other benefits. Leaving the HEAT Lifestyle surely helps with that.

Poor dating = neediness, unnecessary touching, too many compliments, jumping too quickly from one phase to another, becoming love sick, falling to defeat alpha males of the group, lack of confidence, poor looks, poor material game, lack of proper approach mentality, fear of rejection.

The Ugly = being in your forties, looking back with regrets because you never learned how to be good at dating, or how to deal with people in general. Then you give bad advice to younger males, and screw up their perspective of dating because of your own failures. Then you get divorced, if you were married at all, buy a red convertible, and start looking for your lost youth. People call it mid-life crisis. If this is the first time you've heard about it, do your own research. It is the worst thing possible and easy to avoid.

Learn to enjoy your life and get better at dating in your twenties. Your future wife will thank you for it. No woman wants a forty-year-old husband who has the emotional intelligence of a rock and the social experience of a teenager.

What Type of Girl are You Dating?

I also learned that success is based on the type of girl you meet, and using the right point of view. This is the key in my opinion. There are many types of girls and each one is unique. I've never been a fan of generalizing, and I do not advise you to be one either.

Nevertheless, for the purpose of the exercise, I will give you three most common and basic type of girls you meet in you daily life. Let's keep it simple for now.

The Girlfriend One – You can easily spot this girl. She is nice, smiles, usually sexually inexperienced, and shy. Never, never act too needy or too coldblooded with her. Take it very slow and easy, be the lover she needs, and combine it with some first-class gentlemanly behaviour. Speedy strategies do not work here. Until you get in her comfort zone, do not be pushy.

Take it slow and be there for her, and man, she will reward you. Nevertheless, if you are impatient, grow up, and do not lose her just because you are a lazy and impatient ASS (I did it many times, and it SUCKS to see how she is happy with someone else).

The Passionate One - this girl is wild, dancing all the time, talking about sex without fear. She is also quite hot. She usually had a lot of guys around her, and you feel her sexual presence easily. At least two of your friends told you she is a "whore". They are jealous because they could simply not impress her. Weak men do this quite often. Strong men do not generalize and use those nasty, condescending words.

Even if you are right, and the girl is a bit "open-minded",

you should be a gentleman, and remove all those cheap words from your dictionary. Be respectful. After all, if she's sexually free, she might share that with you, and insulting her first won't actually make her like you.

Remember, this type of girl is very selective. She seems to choose her partners, and she looks for the alpha males at the party. I'll put it simply for you – be a lover, the centre of attention, the sexual athlete, the interesting and challenging guy.

But be gentle, use discretion, and be open for anything. She may have unusual, fun tastes. Okay, also from personal experience, girls like this may like kinky things, and if you go to a kink event and dress well and cleanly, you can get a lot of fun possibilities opened up. Fifty Shades of Grey wasn't a success without reason, and learning the good habits from the real community can be very valuable.

The Wrong One - WATCH OUT FOR HER! Any girl including both the girlfriend type and the passionate type can turn into this one. If you come off too aggressively with the girlfriend type she will turn into the wrong one, as this is her defense mechanism. If you act too nice with the passionate one, she will be bitchy, because you are needy and desperate in her eyes. And some girls are purely unsatisfied with life, just as some guys are. So figure that out and stay away.

The wrong type often have been hurt recently, and now they want to destroy the first guy they see. Sometimes they are also barely getting over a breakup and are trying to find a guy who at least looks like their last boyfriend. Either way, this is asking for trouble, so move along.

Elements of Successful Dating

Speaking from experience, a man has to blast through tons

of obstacles in order to be successful at dating. Nothing is handed to us on a silver plate. I have compiled my own list of key elements that will be associated with your dating success.

When reading about them, try to think which ones are natural to you. Which ones do you have or do with ease? Then look closely at the ones that present a challenge. I'd strongly recommend focusing your attention exactly on the elements where you lack experience.

1. **Avatar.** You simply can't attract women if you look like a bum, dress like a bum, or smell like one. Being dressed properly, wearing a nice cologne, following simple soap and water routines, and having an interesting look will give you a big advantage.

Nevertheless, don't forget, the fact that you look good doesn't mean you are good at dating. Consider looks as just the necessary beginning.

2. **Conversation starters.** Having a list of common conversation starters is a big plus. This canned material will help you overcome your fear of approaching with ease.

At some point of time, you will be able to talk to anyone just naturally. Your ability to start a conversation is critical to your success.

3. **Dating routines.** Those routines are your transition from being a cool guy that has the balls to approach, to being an interesting man the girl wants to learn more about. Have a few magic tricks, drinking games, or quick tests you can do, things that no other guy does.

After you have done a few of those, watch for signs of interest. We will discuss those signs of interest in a separate future chapter, as reading them right is quite important.

But use caution and do not overdo it. The goal is to spark an interest, not to look like the local clown or be a doofus. Overdoing quirky things will make the girl think you are showing off, and she will be disinterested in you.

4. **Disinterest and challenge.** We all know how to show interest, but not every guy knows how to keep his distance. Make sure you learn how to be challenging, and learn how to overcome your neediness. Understanding how to act disinterested and not needy will definitely help you in your dating life.

Think about it for a second. Do you present a challenge, or are you a pleaser? We all know that neediness is the one thing that kills attraction immediately. Also, think about your dating heroes – the movie characters that you find effective at dating. Do they look needy, or do they always present themselves as a challenge?

5. **Being the alpha male.** Are you an alpha? If not, make sure you learn how to become one. Being the alpha surely helps when it comes to attracting women.

Ensure you know what being an alpha is. Many bullies think they are alpha males, but in reality, they are not. Alpha males are dominant and strong, but they are also caring and responsible. Lead the way, but remember, the alpha has great power, but also great responsibility. Protecting your friends and taking care of your social circle is an energy-draining job.

6. **List of dating activities.** Make sure you have a list of pre-selected activities and dating routines. Do you know where you can take a girl if a dating opportunity presents itself? Don't tell me about movie theaters, restaurants or coffee shops! Try to be unique in your dating approach.

Take girls to interesting places, where no one else will take them. Some good ideas might be a dance lesson, a painting event, a short road trip, a comedy show, a bookstore or library event, etc. Be creative, be interesting, and be different in a positive way.

7. **Patience.** Man, this is one of the major keys to successful dating. Being patient will get you far. You have to be able to go through those few dates before moving on. Nevertheless, too much patience leads to lack of results or what we call laziness. When it comes to dating, you have to follow the right steps.

Don't rush things, but also do not miss opportunities to advance your relationship.

8. **Common Ground.** This is the concept of having common things to do. You will have hard time establishing comfort with the girl of your interest without having a place to go to or a hobby to do. Common ground will save you from the phone game, because you won't need to call her. You'll just go to your salsa class, for instance, and she will be there, so you can organize everything face-to-face.

Do you go to places where you can meet more women? Are your hobbies helping your dating life?

9. **Wingmen/wing women.** To be an attractive gentleman, you need to have at least one wingman and one wing woman. Your friends can come with you, and will raise your value while socializing, take your attention when you want to look disinterested, advise you, and blast through people who want to interrupt your efforts.

Some guys don't like to share attention with anyone else at a club and will relentlessly cockblock other men. Sometimes the 'best friend' will be jealous and interfere in your dating efforts too. Having a friend who can take care of them while you socialize with desired women is one of the best assets you can have.

Learn to go out together, and always communicate. Tell your wingman what you want him to help you with. Are you doing that on a regular basis?

10. **Interesting stories.** Be interesting, have things to talk about, stories to share, and dreams to discuss. Women love that. You tell them something about yourself, and then they tell you something their life. Then they feel like they've known you for a long time, even within a short period.

Living the HEAT Lifestyle will surely give you tons of experience and you will have quite a few stories to tell. Storytelling is an art of its own. Be an artist!

Once you have all those elements established, your dating life will be so good, you'll be moving on an autopilot. Things will just start happening. You will feel relaxed, confident, and ready to become an expert at dating, and maybe you will meet that significant someone.

We will touch on a lot of those elements in future chapters, and by the end of this book, you will be able to fill in some of your personal gaps with useful skills and motivation.

The Material Aspect of Dating

I have to touch on this, as many, many guys out there have a completely wrong perception about it. You need a good job, a nice car, stylish clothes, clean and interesting place, good looks, excellent grooming, and tons of friends. Period.

A lack of any of the above elements will slow you down, and send you back to the Stone Age. The minute you accept it is the minute you start growing. It sounds shallow, but those are the basic tools you need to be good at dating. It's like doing scuba diving. You just can't dive well with a lack of proper equipment. I was one of these guys that believed the "your personality and your strategy are the only things that matter" concept that many other dating experts will try to sell you. They tried selling it to me too, but I did not buy it.

Try being carless, wearing saggy, unfitting clothes, living in your parents' basement, having no job, being lazy, and tell me how good your dating life is?!

I never, in my entire life, met someone who was really good at dating and avoids the material aspect of it. Yes, don't base your dating primarily on the material aspect of it, or you risk being put into the "provider category". This is fine if you want to be a sugar daddy, but it's not the best for serious dating. But don't forget how important it is to have your life and looks together.

My Advice After This Chapter

To me, dating is a way of living. You need to get constant improvements. Dating is simply to LEARN and HAVE FUN in a polite and respectful way. This is your main goal, and the rest is just part of the experience you are gaining.

In my opinion, dating is the best hobby out there, since it urges you to become better at life in general. My personal point of view is that all of us have a potential to become good at the HEAT Lifestyle and leave something behind. We need practice, effort, and a lot of dedication. The best part is that the more you date, the more confident you get! Good luck!

"I know how to learn anything I want to learn. I absolutely know that I could learn how to fly the space shuttle because someone else knows how to fly it, and they put it in a book.

Give me the book, and I do not need somebody to stand up in front of the class." — *Will Smith*

CHAPTER 9

The Two Biggest and Most Common Challenges We All Have to Face

"There are days that I wake up and I complain, and when I complain, I pinch myself and say, 'that's for complaining.' Not many people can do what they really like in life." — *Enrique Iglesias*

Gentlemen, I think this topic is the most important one so far, since we all get the GAME OVER message from time to time. It sucks when things do not go as planned on a date. Maybe you keep reminding yourself that the dating lifestyle can get messy or tangled. Your emotions might screw you up big time.

Let's look at the two most common challenges that we all

have to go through – the friend zone and lust sickness. Yes, I know this is a very sensitive topic, as we have all failed miserably in both traps, but we have to go over it if we wish to understand how to overcome them. Let me help you out here.

The Friend Zone and How to Avoid It

Let's talk about the friend zone. It is the most dreadful status in the dating lifestyle. Millions and millions of men end up there on a daily basis, and not that many guys understand why they end up there, or how to avoid it. As with everything else, it is a matter of practice and experience.

I know a lot of men who don't end up there anymore, a lot of men who managed to avoid it. What happens is that the girl is convinced your value isn't higher than hers. She doesn't find you to be a potential suitor, a man with status, or a man who can increase her odds of survival and replication. There is no sexual desire at all. Said in simple words, she is not attracted to you as a partner.

Why Does It Happen?

The friend zone is one I personally dislike a lot. You will get in the zone if you have built attraction and have acquired some degree of comfort, but you never escalate to actual seduction. You never move on, and you miss your chance.

Nice guys get to the zone easily, since they show way too much interest and never act challenging, or keep their distance properly. They also lack confidence, and it gets worse with time.

How to Avoid It?

You definitely need to stay challenging and interesting. Do

not lose your vibe, be energetic, and know what comes next. I have personally designed and tested a routine called "3D (3 Dates)", which if followed properly will never lead you to the friend zone. You have to keep those dates under control.

How many times have you gone on endless dates with a girl you liked, just to end up in the friend zone? Maybe you got to hold hands, maybe you got to kiss, but that's all you got. It happened exactly because of those endless dates, with no real progression. Avoid spending too much time with a girl unless you progress naturally. Proper escalation is the key. We will talk about the actual specifics of the successful date in the chapters to come.

If you are looking for a temporary shortcut, and you are in a hurry right now, don't despair. There is also a quick way to avoid it, and the key lies in one simple sentence – I LIKE YOU, YOU ARE COOL, YOU CAN BE MY BEST BUDDY.

Make sure you say it FIRST!

This will reverse the communication model, and present the challenge she is looking for. Now she will ask herself why are you acting like that, don't you like her as something more? This is how you stay interesting and set the grounds first. You only have to say it once. Make sure you say it the first time you meet, before you even get her phone number, before you even ask her out.

This is your VACCINE, THIS IS YOUR SHORTCUT. Use it properly!

What If You End Up There?

Once you are in the zone, it is hard for you to get out. It is hard, because women are evolutionary wired to be attracted to men who will increase their chances of survival and replication, not to guys that are friendly. It will be hard to convince the girl to keep dating you if you failed to trigger attraction every time you meet.

There is something else you can use. If she sees you as a friend, there shouldn't be any problem talking about sex. Not just with her but about sex with other women. You have nothing to lose at this point, so treat her as your buddy. Ask her provoking questions, like "How do you feel about threesomes?" Flirt with her friends, and she will feel like she is losing you. The shitty part is that it usually takes time. Depends on how much time you spend with her.

Use your friendship to hug her and kiss her on the cheeks. Get physically close, but try not to be a creeper. Use discretion and common sense, do not be a douche. The tricky part is to read her body language very well before you attempt anything. Otherwise, you will look like a jackass. Be playful, challenging, and open.

The friend zone is a simple concept, really. When you end up there, you just haven't triggered any attraction switches when you needed to do so. You have spent too much time dating and not moving your relationship any further. You managed to become too nice, too boring, or too common. This is decided early in your dating process. Most likely it is something we have all experienced. Try to understand and accept the facts mentioned above.

Being sent to the friend zone sucks, and no one likes it, but ultimately, it is your responsibility not to get there. Do not blame women for your shortcomings, and if you end up in the zone. You may only blame yourself. The good news is that you have total control over not ending up friendzoned. As I already said, I know a lot of men who do not end up there anymore, and a lot of men who managed to avoid it. I strongly believe you can overcome it too.

Lust Sickness

So, what is Lust Sickness? It is a mental and emotional dependence on one or more girls, which leads to loss of control, emotional breakdown, depression, and mostly DESPERATION. It happens when you get so much in lust with a girl (or two) that you get very needy and dependent on her emotional state.

I say lust, because this is definitely not love. Love is something pure and should be shared, while lust is what gets you in trouble.

Girls are emotional and complicated creatures, and we all know it. They often get entangled and ensnared in their own emotions, then guess who is to blame? That exact guy who is trying to be with her at this very moment. So they drop it on you, start acting bitchy, they refuse your presents, or ignore your attention. They argue with you, tell you stupid shit, and then they get you trapped in an emotional roller-coaster. And not one of those fun ones!

Men are pretty emotional too, and not knowing or being prepared for their own emotions really gets guys caught in that lust trap where they pine after a girl forever. You grow desperate for their attention, and by pushing hard, you only get rejection. You show interest and open desire and expect the same in return. But why do they act like that? Why do you act like that? How come you become so sick of lust that you actually mess it up for both of you? Lust sickness and obsession is what will take you on the certain path to failure...BIG TIME.

Here are the questions we all want to get an answer to:
1. How to prevent yourself from getting sick?
2. How do you overcome it if you get it, or how to heal yourself, without losing the girl?

I've been fighting that disease all my life, until I managed to get to it. Back in the day, I could act as if I didn't care and no one would notice it, but inside, I'd be burning. Don't get me wrong; love is a great feeling, probably the best of them all, but too much love actually feels like an addiction or drug high in the brain, according to studies. It is an addiction with no real physical consequences, but it hurts the most.

How to Prevent Yourself from Getting Sick?

Let's assume you start dating a girl. Think about the following suggestions, as they have proven solid when it comes to preventing yourself from falling badly, and losing control over your emotions:

✓ First, do not put your hopes too high. Don't think that she might be The One. Go after your goals, enjoy life, and do not let yourself obsess. Just approach dating in a fun manner. Relax! Also remember that you are rarely in real love with a girl that you are still chasing. Maybe you have a great attraction to her, but that is not love.

✓ This one is going to help you the most – date as many women as you can. It helps overcome your dependence on women's attention. It gives you a choice, and keeps your raging emotions at a calm state. The more choices you have, the less chance of you falling in lust.

✓ Stop focusing on her. Do not look at pictures of her, do not view her Facebook profile or follow what she does, and do not engage in any action that would have you think about her. Keep up with life and stay busy, or you will start getting overly attached. Don't be neurotic. Dating is fun, but obsessing is not.

✓ If a girl tells you she lost her feelings or starts acting up on you, the best thing is to be COOL. Don't answer, or take your time if you are to answer. Agree with her and show that it does not affect you too deeply. If you get mad or lose control of your temper, there is no coming back. It will also lead to a major fight. You want to avoid that the best way you can, by being neutral about things in the early stages.

How Do You Overcome It If You Get It?

Let's assume you started dating that girl, but all of a sudden, the Lust Sickness overcame you, and you started becoming needy and desperate. You started being a creep who can't control his temper and raging emotions.

Well, it happens, and there are few ways to overcome it:

✓ The very first thing you have to do once you realize you have the Lust Sickness is to stop thinking for few hours. Read a book, watch a movie, play a game. Just relax and escape from reality, because you will damage everything around you. You need to cool down. Do not start analyzing it, or overthinking about it from the very beginning.

✓ Delete every picture from your phone or computer. Unfriend her on social media so you don't have to keep dreaming about having fun with her. Try to erase every physical thing that could remind you of her. Girls do that when they feel the same. I learned it from a girl friend of mine. Eliminate the trigger, so that you don't have to visually be reminded of that bad feeling.

✓ If you realize at some point you actually love her, but it is still early in your dating process – well, you can't prevent the sickness then, but you can shorten the period. The best way is to share with some close friend of yours. Maybe a girl that you consider a friend. Girls are particularly good at this, and they will understand your feelings. Sharing relaxes your mind and heart a lot. Think about other stuff, go to a party, or just go outside (no nostalgic walks in the park allowed).

✓ Take notes of the outbursts. You can easily spot them as you become irrational, emotional, and needy. Count them, take stats, and after few days, try to reduce them. You have to know how often you get it.

✓ Call another girl and just talk to her about other things. Do not share it with her. Just have a normal convo about how she is feeling, what she's doing... listen for a bit.

Remember, the lust sickness is not actually LOVE, but what your need for love causes you to become. LOVE is a great feeling that everybody should experience. I can proudly say that I am in love and it is great. What is even better is to know that the person next to you loves you back.

Make sure you are self-aware, as you need to have pretty high emotional intelligence to be able to avoid getting lust sick. With time, and maturity those things start coming more naturally to you.

My Advice After This Chapter

If you can remember one thing from this chapter, it should be that the best way to become BORING and to be left behind, is to become a hapless SLAVE of your own EMOTIONS. Those blinded with LUST are by destiny ENSNARED. Avoid being needy and demanding, and try to progress the relationship at the right pace – not too fast, not too slow. I hope this book will give you a hint or two on how to make it happen smoother than before.

"Man is free; yet we must not suppose that he is at liberty to do everything he pleases, for he becomes a slave the moment he allows his actions to be ruled by passion". — Giacomo Casanova

CHAPTER 10

A Note on Dress Code and Style

"Fashion fades, only style remains the same". — Coco Chanel

I have put a lot of research into this topic, because a lot of men screw this up. I'm still not sure why, but for some reason style and grooming is considered a "girl's thing" in western societies. The common school of thought is that men should not understand quite well what style is.

Isn't it weird? Why should being clueless be a good thing?

So, if this is the common understanding of how important style is, why do attractive men in movies, books, and TV shows always look really good? Don't you want to stand out too? Yes, you do. That's probably one of the reasons you got this book in the first place. Let me dig into the idea of style.

The cruel reality is that a girl's very first impression comes from your style/looks, approximately three to five seconds after she sees you.

Your clothes can give her many hints and cues about who you are (or about whom you want to be perceived). She will notice that you choose carefully what you wear. She might even make assumptions about you without knowing it on the conscious level.

You will be perceived as sexy, boring, or creative depending on the venue you are in, and what you have decided to wear.

I have summarized all I was able to find and only kept the useful information. I'd like to put some extra insights of my own that you may relate to.

Here Are Some Suggestions:

✓ Make sure your belt, shoes, watch, and hat match. IT IS A MUST. Sometimes there are exceptions to the rule, but man, this is Rule #1 in style in my opinion. How many times have you seen people wearing brown shoes with a black belt, grey socks, and green shirt? This is the most simple and basic rule of fashion, and no one past the age of sixteen should neglect it. Period.

✓ We all know men tend to check out women from top to bottom. Women are the complete opposite. They scan you from bottom to top meaning that your shoes are the first thing they will see. Shoes are very important. In the world of business, people look at your shoes first to check whether they are clean, polished, and well suited with the rest of your outfit. Same principle applies to dating.

✓ Buy nice clothes that fit you and look good based on your body type. Do not pay attention to the price, as price and style are often misunderstood concepts. How often do you see a guy dressed in super-expensive clothes which do not fit him well? I see it all the time, every day. Some guys buy expensive clothes just to show off. The fact that the clothes are expensive does not mean the guy is dressed well. I hate seeing guys that wear cool and expensive clothes which don't match at all. And these guys quite often think they are so cool. NO, THEY ARE NOT. WOMEN NOTICE THAT SHIT. Wear things that suit your body type and personality!

✓ One thing that I wanted to spend more time on is the fact that I keep hearing people complain dressing up well is awfully expensive. No, it is not. It is all in your head. Let me tell you something from personal experience. I came to Canada when I was eighteen with twenty dollars in my pocket. My parents had no money because they had to cover rent and other house related expenses. I had to pay thirty thousand dollars for school over the course of the next four years. My knowledge of the language was limited, and I had no friends or connections. I had to go through eighteen jobs, from being a security guard to painting, roofing, bartending, and tree-planting. I did a lot of shitty jobs because I had to pay my school bills and keep a decent lifestyle.

✓ All through that time, I kept my grooming and dress code to a desired level. I found ways to buy "expensive" clothes the "inexpensive" way. I used to go to Winners, or to my local outlet plaza, and search for sweet deals. If there is a will, there is a way. So, money should not be a problem. If a poor immigrant kid at the age of eighteen could still manage great style ideas in addition to his crazy school expenses, then it should be an easy fix for everyone else.

✓ Remember the basic visual rules of style. Clothes with horizontal lines make you look WIDER, BIGGER IN THE SHOULDERS AREA, and SHORTER. Really tall and skinny people should wear exactly that pattern. Clothes with vertical lines make you look TALLER, SLIMMER, and MORE ELEGANT. These are some simple visual perception rules that I learned when I was in Arts School.

✓ Props and accessories are far more important than you'd think. I started wearing a necklace when I go to clubs or parties. Then girls always asked me about it. Again, I don't wear a necklace every other guy would wear, but something interesting and wild, such as an animal tooth, talon, or a key. I'm adventurous, and this item portrayed my wild side very well. A nice watch, wristband, or any other item that matches your outfit will make you stand out.

✓ Get out there and learn what colors look good on you, what doesn't, and what make you the center of attention. You skin/eyes/hair color should be the critical factors when deciding. For me, red is the best color as, girls have told me so on many occasions. It is followed by black, white, and grey. I noticed that about myself after a lot of observations, trial and error. One thing you should be aware of is that black makes you look slimmer and it shows your definition, while white makes you look bigger/larger. Women know this rule quite well. Ask any of them about it and you will be surprised what you will learn. Also, do this test for me, will you? Put a white sock on you left foot and a black one on the right. Then compare them. I will bet your feet will look shockingly different. One will look bigger than the other, and guess what, it's the white one.

✓ Now, I am exploring this topic past dress code and moving into grooming. You might want to remove all excess hair – nose, ears and whatever. Have a sexy and modern haircut. Acne and yellow teeth are bad, and this should be a common sense. An average-looking man who takes care of himself is often more attractive than a good-looking man who is a slob. Simply put, just be well-groomed. Take care of yourself and it will bring you its rewards.

✓ Stay clean, shower often, and buy nice cologne. No, buy at least three nice colognes, and use them often. A hint of cologne is classy. The rule I follow is ONE spray. That is enough. A li'l bloop on one wrist, smoosh 'em together; neck, neck, side, side. And honestly, a tiny bit of cologne is sexy when one gets close enough.

✓ Probably the most important rule when it comes to style is to have MANY STYLES. Your clothes have to match not only you, but the venue or event you are in. If you are going to a "wine and cheese" event, you can't show up in shorts, or if you are going to the beach you can't put on hair gel and a dress shirt. I've seen some people do the last one, and many others do the first one. Dress accordingly. At the end of the day if you can afford it, and it looks good on you, then buy it. You want your clothes to fit you, not to look like they just fell on top of you, or that your mom bought them for you. Again, you want to buy clothes from nice stores. And if the stores in the malls are too pricy for you, go find some outlets. Clothes are cheap nowadays.

✓ If I can recommend something here, it is to take girls to do some shopping with you. You will learn a lot about style, by doing it on a regular basis. I'd recommend you do it once a month for a year, and only buy one piece of clothing at a time. No need to spend a fortune here, even a shirt will do it. When that year ends, you will be ten times more knowledgeable on the subject of style, as this is an area where you can learn a lot from women. Also, it presents a great "innocent date" opportunity. Then take them home to try the clothes on. This is a great routine. I've seen my friends do it all the time.

It goes like this: let's go shopping...I like this shirt. I'm going to buy it. Let's go home so I can put that on...oh, it looks good on you...oh, you have a sick body...Aw, thanks. Say, you look tired, let me give you a massage...I'll leave the rest to your imagination.

My Advice After This Chapter

I want you to remember one thing. Style is indeed important. After all, a well-groomed guy that is dressed nicely will have far better response from women than some guy who has no clue about dress codes. Looks are only critical in the beginning, but if you can't get through the beginning, what is the point of that great personality you have to offer?

Being well-dressed often is considered a sign of high self-esteem too. Don't let yourself forget that!

"Physical elegance, which is what I am talking about here, comes from the body. This is no superficial matter, but rather the way that man found to honour the way he places his two feet on the ground." — Paulo Coelho

CHAPTER 11

Common Ground

"Find what you love and let it kill you." — *Charles Bukowski*

As I have already mentioned, the easiest way to meet new people it to get involved in social activities, or to visit places where people gather on a regular basis. This is what I like to call having a common ground.

I experienced the power of the common ground twenty years ago, in my early high school years. I noticed that if you want to have a lot of friends, you need to do a lot of different things. At the end of my senior high school year, I was already the captain of our debating team, I was involved in multiple Youth Red Cross youth activities, I'd had three photo exhibitions, and I was heavily involved in the local Ecology Club. I had an event to attend every week, I had concerts to host, competitions to organize, projects to work on, training seminars to attend, and photography contests I needed to win. Was it ever fun!

Common Ground Examples

Having common ground definitely did miracles for me, and I've experienced its influence over my life ever since. It is a well-known fact that the best way to meet people with certain interests is to get involved. I lived in few European and few North American cities, and I always used that principle. Many of these activities tend to have high female-to-male classmate ratios, and doing something that other guys won't call 'manly' can actually give you an edge. Dance, fitness, and cooking classes tend to be girl-heavy so everyone ends up wanting to pair with the guy. Even if guys go to the classes looking for girls, and the girls know it, they're still interested partly because of numbers. A guy doesn't have to be a gorgeous stud to get attention, and guys with less conventional good looks can go really far here, although grooming habits are a must. Women aren't stupid, they know why guys hang out with lots of girls, but still, they're definitely down for a guy who's not afraid to be around and hang out with girls.

✓ **Dance Classes.** One of the best places to meet girls. You can't dance? So what? Go out there and learn, and don't be afraid to have fun. Tango, salsa, bachata classes...I've never seen places with so many good-looking girls per square foot.

✓ **Clubs/Bars/Coffee Shops.** They are quite busy, they have high concentrations of good-looking girls, and everyone goes there. If you are in your twenties, you should be going out every week, or at least twice a month.

✓ **Cooking Courses.** There's nothing better than inviting a girl over and cooking together. But wait; you have no idea how to cook. Open Google and sign up for a cooking class.

Besides learning how to be patient and make tasty food, you will meet a lot of quality women.

✓ **Group Fitness Activities.** Great for your general health, and incredible for your social life. A lot of girls prefer going to the group class activities compared to going just to the gym. Do a Google search and see which group fitness classes are hot these days. Spin classes? Cross fit? Yoga?

✓ **Arts/Drawing Events.** Do you like painting? Then this is the perfect place for you. They are quite popular nowadays. You don't like to draw? Then go anyway. Unlocking your inner artist is never a bad idea, and learning to relax is very valuable. Remember, you don't have to be good, but taking a risk will make you attractive. Women love artists. Remember what Leonardo Di Caprio did in Titanic? Drawing got him far.

✓ **Wine Tasting.** If you like classy women or you want to be perceived as a true gentleman, these are perfect. You need to know your wines. Plus, women love wine too. You might also want to take another note here. ALWAYS HAVE A BOTTLE OF WINE AND SET OF CANDLES AT HOME. I believe I don't need to explain that any further.

✓ **Volleyball/Beach volleyball.** Amazing experiences, tons of fun, and lots of girls!

✓ **Language classes.** Do you want to be able to speak to hot Latin women when you go on you next vacation at the Caribbean? Or maybe you like women that want to learn Spanish just like you. Sign up! You will meet a lot of new people, and you will expand your communication skills in another language.

✓ **Universities/Colleges.** We all know you met most of your best friends through school. We all did. If you are going to university or college, please take advantage of it and be social. Most of you will be there for few years, so don't waste time; go out and make friends.

✓ **Ski/Snowboard/Ice skating classes.** If you enjoy the winter and you love the outdoors, then why not try meeting new people at the closest mountain resort?

✓ **Sports tournaments.** If you like watching sports or you are a part of a local team, them I've got good news for you. You will meet a lot of people. I used to play water polo for my University of Ottawa team, and I had a blast when we went to a tournament in another city.

✓ **Volunteering.** This is a big one. Let's put it this way – you meet a lot of people by helping people. Makes sense? You may also find an organization which works with kids. Learning to be fun and interesting to kids is a skill you will need later in life.

✓ **Photography.** Women love photography. They love to see other people adore them. They love their looks, and when self-conscious about their looks, can be very validated by artistic appreciation. So why are you not attending a photography class yet? Buy a nice camera.

Benefits of Common Ground that You Should Consider

When I was younger, I used my desire to meet people combined with my adventurous personality to turn my social life into the kind most guys my age dream about. I had so many friends from so many clubs, schools, and NGOs, that when I went out, familiar people were saying "hi" to me every ten minutes.

It was insane how social I became from my involvement in different activities around the city. Here are some of the benefits of having a Common Ground:

✓ **Isolated group.** For instance, attending a salsa class leaves you room to work with a smaller group. You have fewer obstacles to overcome, you have less people to mess it up for you. It is a segregated group, and you should take advantage of the fact that you are together on a regular basis.

✓ **Less competition.** In that group of people, there are no ex boyfriends, no jealous bffs, no pressure from already existing social sources. I'm not saying you will be totally unimpeded, but you are definitely away from all the daily drama that your love interest's social circle may contain.

✓ **Easier to approach.** Do you have approaching anxiety? Are you facing challenges approaching people you don't know? Well, having a Common Ground will almost get rid of that fear. Working in smaller groups, you always have the chance to start a conversation much more easily than if you had to do it in a club, or at a random event. In most cases, you will even have to introduce yourselves to the group. How great is that?

✓ **Repeated meetings/dates.** Think about it. You don't have to call to meet up, you don't have to be ensnared by the text game, and you don't need to arrange dates. You know that every Tuesday at 8 and every Thursday at 7 there is a class or a meet up. If you like a girl, and you are attending the same seminar or a class, then you have much higher chances to see her quite often without any effort. Shortcut? Oh yeah.

✓ **Opportunity to turn a class into a date.** Do you want to learn more about the girl you have interest in? Do you want to raise your social value, and show her how much you have to offer? Do you don't want to spend hundreds of dollars on useless dates? Well, brother, here is your chance. Sign up and use every meeting as an opportunity to learn more about her, and to build more comfort.

✓ **Easier to get out for an actual date.** This about it this way. You have spent some time together, and you've learned about each other in a non-needy way. How much easier will it be to take the girl from your course on an actual date compared to the girl you just met at the club last Friday?

✓ **Shared interests.** You don't want to just meet some girl. You want to meet a girl you can have fun with, who shares similar interest with you. Right? Then the best way is to do something you enjoy, which can be enjoyed by girls too. Stay away from guys-only activities if you want to meet girls.

My Advice After This Chapter

You probably want to know how to take full advantage of the Common Ground you chose. Well, it is this simple – find something you would like doing, sign up, and enjoy it!

Now the real question is, do you go to places where you can meet more girls? Are your hobbies helping your dating life? Take a pen and paper and do a simple exercise. Write five interests your dream girl has. Examples are, but not limited to – she likes to read, she likes sports, she likes to party, she likes nature, she likes winter, she likes to dance, she likes the beach, etc.

Then besides each of those five interests, write a common ground. If she likes to read, then bookstores, libraries, young writers' clubs, and literature events will be great examples. If she likes to dance, then salsa classes, hip-hop seminars, and Zumba events will be your thing.

Got it? You start from a single interest and then you expand to an activity, event, or a class you could attend.

Bear in mind, if you like to play "grease monkey" and enjoy spending countless of hours fixing your car, attending an auto mechanics course might not be the best way to meet women. Try to choose activities that apply to wider range of people, rather than doing something that only a guy would do, or something in your comfort zone.

Then, once you sign up, make every visit count. Increase the level of interest people have for you, build rapport with more people, get dates, and have fun!

"Being alone never felt right. Sometimes it felt good, but it never felt right." — Charles Bukowski, Women

PART III

Master the Art of Dating While Living the Dream

CHAPTER 12

Starting a Conversation Without Looking Like a Tool

"You have to enjoy life. Always be surrounded by people that you like, people who have a nice conversation. There are so many positive things to think about." — *Sophia Loren*

Ever since I was a little boy, I've been gifted with the ability to talk to people openly without any fear. I started talking when I was thirteen months old and I never stopped after that. 13 months, that's a year and one month! Not to brag about it, but most kids barely make sounds at that age, while I was completing full sentences, asking questions and generally having lots of fun with my newly acquired skill – talking.

It took me more than thirty years after that to realize that listening is a far superior skill. Confident people know how to listen!

Being a gifted talker, but a poor listener, I excelled at starting conversations through my entire life, and I had a lot of fun doing it. However, that didn't mean I wasn't shitting my pants every time I had to approach a beautiful woman.

Oh yes, I did. We all get it: the shakes, the dry mouth, the sweating. The adrenaline rushes through us, and turns us into speechless logs.

And again, as with everything else in life, it is a matter of understanding and experience. I know for a fact that approaching is one of the easiest things to do if you are properly prepared. Let's dig into it.

Fear of Approaching and How to Overcome It

Here's my advice – rejection/being turned down is not necessarily based on personal failure. Sometimes people just aren't attracted to you/don't feel that way about you, and that's okay. Always keep that in mind, and be cool if you get rejected.

What I have learned from my friends is that the fear of approaching comes from the fact that you don't know what to say, not from the approach itself.

Do me a favor and go to a museum. Stand before a painting you are seeing for the first time, and try to talk to the person staring at it. This will suck. Now, try to research the concept behind the art, read about that specific exhibition, about the painter, and learn the story behind each painting. Then go again. The conversations will spark and catch fire because you are prepared.

That being said, learning more about women and understanding their interests will definitely help you approach with ease. Knowledge is power, as the saying goes.

The approach, being the first step of meeting someone, requires you to be unique and interesting. There are few key points that will get you mind set the proper way.

I'll outline them, as well as the most commonly made mistakes:

1. Have a pre-set conversation starter for multiple situations and locations. That is the hard one. If I see a girl on the bus, I ask for directions. If I see a girl in the club, I ask her something about her friend next to her, etc. The conversation starter should be simple, interesting and cool. YOU MUST HAVE AT LEAST ONE! Be ready. But guess what? I have a separate chapter coming up that just focuses on conversation starters. It will give you some basic ideas and examples.

MISTAKES: People move in and say something stupid, the girl looks serious, and the guy gives up right away. The guy moves in and says nothing, just lingers around her acting like she has to start the conversation. Been there, done that.

2. Do not hesitate, and start talking. Thinking too much before approaching will only increase your fear, and you will end up not doing anything. When you have a list of conversation starters and you see a girl you like, go for it right away.

MISTAKES: Waiting too long, so someone else can move in. Also, thinking way too much about which conversation starter to choose. Again, go for it; do not wait. Train yourself to follow that rule. It will save you a lot of headaches down the road; plus, you will be faster than most guys.

3. Start the conversation, be interesting and challenging, and then leave. I like to take off soon after I start the conversation. I do not like lingering. Go in, make the impression, and remember to give a fake time constraint. Tell them you won't be there for more than two seconds, and do leave soon. This will get you out of the "needy basket". When you come back later for a second conversation, the girl will be already open to talk to you. This makes things much easier for you.

MISTAKES: Not giving a fake time constraint. She sees you as a nasty, dirty bum that wants to bother her all night long. Remember you can never go wrong by leaving too soon if you have made a positive impression. Be the cool guy that likes to socialize, not the creep that stalks women and clings to them.

4. Stop thinking or caring about rejection. Approaching is not dating. Approaching is 1% of dating. The outcome just doesn't matter. As long as you move out quickly the point is taken. I'd strongly recommend you see approaching as something fun, rather than something at which you must succeed at every time. Go talk to people for no reason. Learn not to be emotionally dependent when approaching.

MISTAKES: People start thinking, 'OMG, she will cut me off, and what will I do then?' Some guys think about it way too much. Others are care about the result way too much. If you just met the girl, why are you so serious? Just because she's attractive doesn't mean she's your first or last chance at love, or even getting laid. Drop your expectations, please. Have fun.

If you take those key points into consideration properly, your approach anxiety will disappear almost completely.

When you see a girl you like, do not start thinking of

excuses not to approach – she's too hot, she'll never talk to me, or it's not the right time, or I'm not dressed properly. This is just an excuse and will get you nowhere. Instead, think that ten other guys saw that girl and thought that she is too good for them. You are going to be different.

Easy to Use Conversation Starters

Following the previous pages, I will try to outline some really good conversation starters that my friends and I have tried over the years.

Remember that to fight your fear of approaching, you may need to have pre-set phrases that you can use to start a conversation. Then eventually you will become natural at this and your conversation starting skills will not require any pre-set material. You will just be so much more confident!

Please do me a favor and forget about the term "pickup line".

This term is used by guys who have 0% knowledge of the dating game. It is lame, it is weak, and it shows you have no more class and knowledge than a confused teenager. The minute I hear someone ask me, "hey, what is your best pickup line?" is when I know this guy has no clue about dating.

Problem is, we often want the one-shot-score – use one line and make all the girls yours. Well, good luck with that attitude. The only thing a conversation starter does is to get the conversation started. That's all. It is nothing more, nothing less.

A one-liner could not, and will not get you the girl!

Thinking otherwise makes you a huge, clumsy tool. So let's forget that awful term, 'pickup line', and use the term 'conversation starter'. Most importantly, let's talk about starting a conversation the proper way.

Let's first look at the Big NOs:

1. Do not approach random girls on the street, and do not play the cold approach game. This is creepy, and will get you arrested.

2. Do not ever start a conversation with "hi, my name is". In fact, do not ask about her name unless she asks first. When she does, make her guess it by giving her the first letter. Play with it.

3. Do not ever try the "can I buy you a drink" conversation starter. This is the worst conversation starter you can use. It shows neediness and insecurity, and suggests that there is nothing interesting about you. A girl will see you as a sponsor right away, take the drinks, and never talk to you again.

4. Do not start a conversation with a compliment – "Oh, you have nice shoes, hair, body, dress, etcetera". It has the same effect as the one above – it turns you into a sleazy bum. You will give compliments at a later time when you start dating. For now, stick to being interesting and challenging.

5. Try not to use the word "sorry". "Sorry, can I ask you something", "Sorry, sorry, sorry, can I talk to you", etc. Sorry = Needy. Try replacing it with something positive and more enthusiastic.

6. Do not talk to the girl by facing her directly or coming too close. Try talking over your shoulder, or approach her at an angle. Leave the face-to-face conversations for later. This is less intense, more casual, and creates interest.

7. If you like a girl and she has friends around, do not go straight for her. Approach and talk to her friends instead. Let her come after you for attention. Win her social circle before you win her.

8. Do not look afraid, confused, or desperate. SMILE, or have a NEUTRAL expression. If you are not sure how to do it properly, try looking yourself in the mirror more often. Get a better idea of what your facial expression communicates.

9. If the conversation does not spark well, or it dies at some point of time, do not stay there and look awkward. Say "I have to join my friends," and excuse yourself. Continuing to bother a lady who's clearly not interested is like talking louder and slower to people who don't speak English. It accomplishes nothing besides making you look like a jackass.

10. Do not wait for other guys to approach first, do not overthink it, and do not wait way too long before you approach.

Do any of the above, and your chances of getting her number, or even her name, are high. Believe me, girls get approached every day, and guys use the same lame approach techniques above. Avoiding dumb mistakes is a critical part of your learning process. However, do not judge yourself too harshly if you have been doing some or all of the above up until now. It's a learning process, and forward momentum is the important part.

The purpose of this book is to open up your eyes for things that you are not doing right, and then to help you learn how to be better at dating.

When it comes to starting a conversation, I personally like asking for an opinion, since it seems like you want to learn something. There are many more conversation starters out there that you can use, but the point is to just start talking, and that's all. It's that simple.

As you will see, the PRINCIPLE behind conversation starters is quite simple. See the example below:

1. What is the best music for a workout? (First, go with the question conversation starter)
2. My buddy, who's a DJ, told me I should listen to a music that has the pace of the exercise I'm doing. (You make a statement and then pause)
3. Do you think [this band] is cool? I'm still not so sure about it...(Followed by another question)

Got the logic behind it? A good conversation starter is not a one liner, but rather a whole, short script.

Examples That You Might Like

Here is my personal list of conversation starters for different situations, gathered from a lot of trial and error. Again, there are so many more ways to start a conversation, but the conversation starters below should at least give you a perspective of how it works.

- ✓ Do you think summer is the best season to meet new friends? (Pause). I read this article in a magazine and they said spring and fall are better. What do you think?
- ✓ Is kissing cheating? (Pause). I keep arguing with my friends over there, and I need a girl's opinion.
- ✓ OMG, wow (Pause). Are they real? She replies, "What?" Your nails look so...(Pause) different. You know, my sister loves that color, but she says it doesn't look good on most people. But you're really pulling it off!

- ✓ Why black (red, white, tiger, yellow, referencing what she is wearing)? (Pause). I gotta stay away from you (Pause). People say girls who wear black are pretty rebellious. What do you think?
- ✓ Drinking a cocktail is cool, but can you handle a real drink? (Let her say something). Okay, I'll let you practice a bit more with that fancy straw and I'll be back later to find out if you can handle something stronger. (Smile and leave, come back later with few shots).
- ✓ Do you think dieting works? I went to a diet specialist and they told me I have to eat smaller meals four to five times a day, instead of three big ones. (Pause). How about dinner and breakfast? I think breakfast should be big meal, while dinner should be just something simple...
- ✓ Pick a napkin, draw a #, and put an X somewhere (tic tac toe style). Go to the girl at the bar, put it in front of her and say "Your turn!" (Play and have fun. If she wins, ask for a rematch).
- ✓ Hey guys I can only stay for a minute before I gotta get back to my friends, but I need a female opinion on something. When a girl makes out with a guy at a club and she has a boyfriend, it is considered cheating?
- ✓ Do you think guys should shave their chest? (Pause) A bodybuilder friend of mine told me that if I want to go to the beach and look COOL, I should do it. What do you think?
- ✓ Can you swim well? (Pause). I'm trying to teach my little cousin to swim, but he's afraid of water. Why do people fear water so much?
- ✓ Don't you hate this? (Pause). She replies "what?" Then you could say "Look, that girl is staring at that guy. She totally wants him, but it's too awkward to approach, everyone sees her everyone hears her..."

✓ What's the best sun lotion? I asked my friend, and she works in a tanning salon, and she told me it has to be at least 35 SPF+ for good protection. How about if you have a darker skin? Should I wear stronger lotion?

✓ Your sister looks too serious. (Pause). She replies "she is not my sister". And you answer with "Oh wow, you look like you are related. I got fooled for a second. I noticed your body language is quite the same. How do you know each other?"

✓ Hi. I'm being sent on a mission. One of my friends wants to know if you are a good dancer. (Pause). We had an argument. I thought you were at least decent at dancing. He thinks you are really good." She replies, "I'm really good," or, "I'm okay." I can't tell unless I see it, but I gotta get back to my friends (at this point you leave, have a drink, and come back, inviting her to the dance floor).

✓ Last but not least, a bold conversation starter for those who believe they have the confidence to pull it off. You see a girl at the bar. You walk over, and ask over your shoulder, "What should I drink?" She replies "what?" "You probably get a lot of free drinks, so you have to know what's really good down here. Advise me! But be creative!"

There is one thing that works very well during daytime and sometimes at night too. It only works well if the girl of your interest can hear you from a distance.

Say something, use your selected conversation starter, and then don't look her in the eyes, but in an imaginary direction. Keep talking to her and finish your sentence. Be like James Bond and act as if you are busy thinking about something else, look in other direction but still talk to her. Pay attention to her with your peripheral vision. Girls notice that. Then smile and look her in the eyes. Keep talking from there.

I've done that many times, and strangely enough, it works really well. This conveys confidence, and calm relaxed personality. But watch out, because some more insecure girls will consider an overly-confident guy intrusive.

My Advice After This Chapter

As you know, starting a conversation is the first step to the dating process. Some people are good at it, while others, not so much. If approaching really freaks you out, and you start shaking and you feel insecure, and the situation is really that bad, then start slowly. We all have that same fear, remember? You could start talking to people you meet for practice, whether or not you're attracted to them.

Start asking questions and showing interest to people in general, not just girls. Start talking. Start learning about communication by communicating openly with a lot of people. This will help you fight the fear of approaching and turn you into communication expert.

Consider getting a sales/retail job for the sake of learning. Most companies that hire sales/retail specialists offer pretty good training. That training will be quite useful, as it provides the fastest and the best way to overcome your approach anxiety.

When I say a sales job, I mean a real, corporate/retail sales job. Stay away from cold-calling/door-to-door types of jobs. You will hear more about those specific jobs in the next short chapter.

When you get good at starting conversations, try to make up your own conversation starters based on the situation you are in. Keep it cool, simple, and engaging.

Try to be smooth. If you see a girl reading an interesting

book, ask for it. If you see a girl in the club looking at you, go and say her staring is creepy, but you'll let her buy you a drink. If you go to a party, go on and just say "Hi", and ask the girls how they know the host. Learn to be creative and spontaneous, but not creepy or overly personal. After all, it's all about becoming natural at dating while having fun. Did I mention not to be creepy?

In the end remember, if you don't believe in yourself, no one will. You need to have CONFIDENCE, CONFIDENCE, and a bit more CONFIDENCE!

"After about twenty years of marriage, I'm finally starting to scratch the surface of what women want. And I think the answer lies somewhere between conversation and chocolate." — Mel Gibson

CHAPTER 13

Building Interest, Presenting a Challenge, and Leaving a Positive Impression

"I know I'm incredibly unpredictable, and that's the only thing I'm sure of." — *Sylvester Stallone*

"Humor is mankind's greatest blessing." — *Mark Twain*

What should happen after you start the conversation? Show me the big picture!

Okay, here is my example. For the sake of the exercise, let's assume I met a girl in a bar, or at a party.

After I approach and start the conversation, I usually move to my interest building routines right away. My goal is to show her, I'm fun, interesting, challenging, and that I'm so unique and different that the other guys. Here is what I personally do:

1. I do one of my interest-building routines.

2. Then I spice up the conversation with mixed questions, stories, opinions, and role playing. I talk about interesting thing most of the time; nothing conventional, nothing common, nothing that all other guys talk about. I'd warm her up with some opinion questions. Example: Who cheats more, guys or girls? What is your favourite part of a man's body? Which personality traits do you like in a guy? What do you hate in a guy (ohhhh some negative reinforcement)?

3. Then I will isolate the girl from the group, maybe take her to the bar, or to a nice empty table in the club/bar. I will follow up by finding her on Facebook, and looking at her pictures together. The fun starts when I begin making light, but funny jokes depending on what I see there. I will tease her for a bit. Maybe do some more role playing.

4. By that time, I'll know what type of a girl she is. Remember one of the previous chapters? If she is the WRONG ONE, I'd try being funny and show significant amount of confidence, I'll be borderline cocky. If she is the GIRLFRIEND TYPE, I'll start telling her my love stories from the past (mostly mistakes, of course) to build trust. I will not go into much detail, but I will make it look like I learned few things from my past relationships. If she is a PASSIONATE ONE, I will move on directly to talking about what she likes in bed, what is her favourite position (doggy, usually). Then I will indirectly share stories about being sexually active and experienced.

5. Then I will kiss her. I also tend to show more physical interest at this point. I pick her up, I arm-wrestle with her,

and I dance with her. It also helps with discouraging all the other jerkoffs who are trying to impress the same girl.

What happens when you run out of things to say, or if the girl is accustomed to it and now ignores it? You demonstrate higher value in order to build attraction, and you try to look interesting.

But sometimes, when you keep going, it's too much. You show off and look like a clown. She feels like she's LOST the CONTROL and she refuses to take it anymore. Bombard her with attention in the attraction phase, but then slow down.

Try to always use humour if you mess it up somewhere. I have learned that lesson the wrong way far too many times. Be smarter than I was. Let's focus on two major concepts for a second – how to identify if a girl is interested in you by her body language, and how to present a challenge yourself.

How to Identify Interest

Have you been wondering if a girl will speak to you if you approach her, or if she is going to kiss you back, or have sex with you? Identifying interest is one of the hardest challenges most guys have. Most girls are pros when it comes to reading us. Girls are raised to be better at communication and understanding human behaviors then us.

On another note, most of us are not really hard to read. Most guys are too direct and way too obvious when it comes to attraction. This is the main reason every guy needs to learn how to present a challenge. Being challenging will help you stand out from the other Neanderthals in the venue.

✓ **She smiles at you for more than few seconds.** A woman's smile is a direct indication that you should get your ass up and go talk to her. The smile is one of the basic flirting techniques, and its purpose is to attract attention, so don't be shy – smile back and go talk to her!

✓ **She passes by you in the club several times and keeps walking around you for no apparent reason.** Most likely, the reason is you. She is trying to get noticed.

✓ **She attracts attention to her lips and mouth** – she plays with the straw of her drink, she touches her lips, etc. A woman's lips are very seductive, and she knows that.

✓ **She isolates herself.** After you made eye contact, she keeps some distance between her friends, practically inviting you to go talk to her (don't worry this won't happen very often).

✓ **She mimics your movements, unintentionally of course.** When you laugh, she laughs or smiles, if you dance, she dances as well.

✓ **She plays with her hair, earrings, or glasses.** This is probably the easiest way to recognize interest. If she touches her hair, or pets it, it is certain that she's showing interest in you!

✓ **She touches you unintentionally, or so it seems.** She breaks the physical barrier and knows that this will get you out of control. This is a very strong indicator of interest.

✓ **She makes eye contact.** It is said that the eyes are a window to the soul. Weather it is true or not, making eye contact shows trust. Do not break the eye contact if it happens. Try to see who will break it first, you or her.

✓ **She invades your personal space**. She asks direct questions about your past, poking at old relationships, etc. She wants to know you, because she is really interested in you. My advice is stay away from directly answer those questions, as this is also her testing how compliant you are. In the beginning you want to be challenging, rather than compliant.

✓ **She starts the conversation first.** Well, even a child can tell what that means. Many men will lose interest if a girl approaches them and does most of the work. I don't share this idea. If she approaches you, and you like her, don't be a prick. Talk to her. Even if you're not into her, it's great practice and can be more fun than you'd expect.

✓ **My favorite proof that she is interested is still when she asks about your name.** I don't introduce myself, and I talk and talk until she asks for my name. NICE!

I'd like to put emphasis on something outstandingly important. Most guys see the some of those indicators, and they automatically think the girl is so into them - "OMG, she smiled at me, she wants me so much!"

Remember, building attraction is just the beginning. She is indicating an interest, and that is all; nothing more, nothing less. Don't be cocky and think she is yours, because she is not. It is clearly a sign made specifically for you. It is like a green light, and states: YOU CAN NOW PROCEED! But crossing that intersection is up to you.

How to Present a Challenge

Being challenging is one of the main reasons some men are attractive. Here is a well-known dream: "I want to meet a knight in shining armor on a white horse, someone who will rescue me." This is a social frame that has been implanted in men's heads for ages. We have to be nice to women, we have to praise them, we have to court them, and we have to put them above anything else.

Here is the real dream: "I want to meet a dark knight on a dark horse, a rebel, someone who follows his own rules, and someone that needs a princess to turn him into a prince." Believe it or not, this is what women really look for in a guy. Not a guy to put them on a pedestal, but a rebellious, adventurous man that they can turn into someone good. Take a second to reflect on this one.

Interest is something that can get lost in a second, while it takes a lot of time to build up. You need to know what to say and when to say it. I've seen girls fall for a guy right after he has dropped something stupid and illogical, and I've seen tons of other girls that have pulled away from guys after saying something quite innocent. Go figure.

"Oh, you are so beautiful, you are gorgeous, and you are so HOT". This line will mess up your chances within seconds. Showing so much interest is what most guys do when seeing a girl, but we all know where that leads – the dreaded friend zone.

There are many phrases you can use, but here are just some examples to illustrate what will make you challenging:

1. "I'm not exactly a nice guy. I spend much more time thinking then feeling. I have a lot of passion, but feelings? Nah, not for me. Stay away from me." Now give her a huge smile.

When to say it: The earlier you say it, the better. And it works best when you meet the girl, as an intro to yourself. Make sure you only say it when you have just met. And smile a lot while saying it.

2. "We have to stop here, let's not rush things!"

When to say it: Anytime, while dating, and she shows too much interest. Make sure you say it in a teasing way. Girls use that phrase on us all the time, don't they?

3. "Is there any chance you won't show up, or you'll flake on me? You are not one of those flaky girls are you?"

When to say it: This is a killer move. You do it when you have already arranged a date just to make sure it saves you ass from her flaking. And it does.

4. "I have to stay away from you, I can't hold it, it's so hard...I feel strange around you. Please don't kiss me tonight."

When to say it: When you just meet, and you had few conversations. If she chases you, then she is into you. She'll ask something like, "Why don't you want me to kiss you?" - Credit to the movie Twilight. The movie is questionable in my point of view, but that line works.

5. "You are so nice, and I'm an ASS...I don't deserve you".

When to say it: I've heard so many people, both men and women break up with their partner using this line, and they got away with it. You simply admit you are, who you are, and she will feel the need to fix you.

6. "Are you sure you want to do this, maybe we should stop here if you are not comfortable today!"

When to say it: Say it when you start cuddling and making out on your bed just before you move further. Stop doing what you are doing for a bit and pull that line. It will raise you comfort level with her.

7. "You are so cool. I think we can be really good friends.

Give me a high five. You are like my buddy now. We can go fishing together."

When to say it: Say it any time when you feel the girl is giving you some sort of resistance. Use it any time you meet a girl. Use it as a test. Use it in a text message, or Facebook conversation. Use it to get her interest. Use it a while before you actually start going on dates.

8. "You really need to work on your kissing!" (Said in a playful tone, and then laugh together.)

When to say it: After you kiss for the first time, drop that line. She is surely going to kiss you for a second time.

These examples might seem unreasonable at first, and you might say "I'll never say that to a girl." If that is your opinion, I'm strongly recommending you that you field test them. Practice makes perfect. You have to train yourself to say them properly and at the right moment. They are fearless, they are illogical, they seem cheesy, but they build attraction like nothing else. That's what matters.

Also, take a note of the following fact. If you are shown interest and you do not proceed further, then you are a loser in girl's eyes. Ignoring her interest for too long is a dangerous move. You might often ignore them to make her chase you, but know the limits. Always reward a girl's interest with your own.

In conclusion, remember that some girls are just not up to meeting guys in general, some girls are not up to meeting any guys tonight, some girls like other girls, some girls have no social skills or confidence, and some girls just get scared too fast.

Don't worry if a certain girl is not giving you any signs of interest. Just move on to the next one and treat this example as practice!

At Last – My Favourite Interest Building Routines

Most guys fear approaching not because they can't start a conversation, but because they have no clue what comes next. It's easy to go and say "Hi, can I get your opinion on something?", but what comes next? How to keep the conversation going?

After I realized that, I started taking notes of what I have done well in the past, and I figured out some pretty good routines and techniques. In the following pages, I will focus on the ones I like the most – tests, short stories, and role playing. At the end of it, we will look at the big picture, or how to actually put them in place.

Tests

My favourite interest builders are the personality test routines. There are so many short and interesting tests out there that you can do in a normal social setting. They can be used any time you want to demonstrate how interesting you are. Reading people's personalities in a creative and inspiring way is what will send your attractiveness through the roof.

By the way, if you play a guitar, you do magic, you talk slowly and deeply, or you make other girls love you, you won't need many other interest-building routines.

This strategy below has been field tested probably a thousand times. It is my favourite. It works so well if you play it right. You would go up to a girl ask her to pick a number from one to ten, and then tell her seven. Then you will elaborate on it, because most people do actually choose seven. It is an old test you can find all over the Internet, and it works. Here it is:

1. After I had started a conversation with a girl and we went back and forth few times, I'd go straight up to her and tell her:

    Me: What do you know about non-verbal communication and body language? (Simple question to trigger her interest)

    Her: (She says something)

    Me: People tend to express their thoughts through their body language, and they often communicate subconsciously using a non-verbal communication. There are two types of people. The first type are very open and their body tells people about everything they're thinking. When it comes to the second type, their body does not tell much. They are more serious and they know how to hold their emotions. 80% of people fit the first group, 20% in the second. Let me see where do you fit? (You look smart, you look sophisticated, and you get her attention and interest just with that paragraph.)

    Her: Tell me, tell me. (She is hooked)

2. Take her hand, do not look her in the eyes, and look at the hand. Start touching the knuckles of each finger; massage the knuckles one by one until you finish with the hand. Be slow. Smile when doing one finger, frown when you touch another. Man, she will get so curious. After finishing with the first hand, get the second and do the same. After you are done, look her in the eyes and say:

    Me: Now, think about a number between one and ten. Thing quick, the first number you can think of, and keep it to yourself. Don't tell me the number.

    Her: Ok, I got it. (Now at this point she is all yours, so take a quick break of fine to ten seconds, have a sip of your drink, say cheers, you are in control).

    Me: Perfect, give me back your hands.

3. You do the same thing with her hands in the same order you did in point two. However, now, you have to act as if things have changed since the last time you touched her. So, your goal is to turn down three fingers. What do I mean? You are touching her knuckles, and all of a sudden, you stumble to a knuckle that feels different. It actually doesn't, but she does not know it.

    So you flip that finger in and just close that finger. The rest stay open. Do the same thing for two other fingers, preferably one on the first hand, two on the second hand.

4. Take a break again, take a sip, and say cheers. Do not let her move or change the way her hands/fingers were. Then you pull out your cell phone and type seven on the display, but do not show it to her yet. Then show it to her and ask her if that is her number. For the record, you have a 70% chance of her selecting seven, so go for it.

5. If you guessed the number, she will think you are some sort of evil genius. She will look stunned, and man, she will be so impressed. Believe me.
    Her: OMG, how did you get it?
    Me: Look at your fingers; they show three down and seven up. Your number is seven.
    Her: How did you know? How come? What happened?
    Me: Magic. I do know how to read people and body language very well.
    Her: Tell me how you did it, please.
    Me: Sorry, but I can't. You are a very nice, open person, and your body language expresses your feelings and thoughts. You are like me. I got my number answered right away.

6. If you do not guess the number, then what? It suck, but man, you can still win her over very easily, because you have protected yourself in the beginning. Thus, you base your strategy on her being unique.
    Her: No, this is not the number.
    Me: What is it?
    Her: Eight (or whatever).
    Me: Well, then you are truly unique person. You fit that 20% of people that cannot be read. You are in very strong control of your emotions. You think with your head. You are probably a very careful person.
    Her: (she smiles)
    Me: I couldn't guess the number for only you and two other people.
    Her: Out of how many?
    Me: Probably a hundred. You might be truly unique. Now you've gotten my interest! Tell me more about yourself. What do you like in a guy?

If she tells you to do it to someone else, you must REFUSE it. Tell her you only do it to people you want to get to know better. You did a test on her, and if you have managed to get the seven, you also did magic, and she will be very curious from now on. Guys, girls love this test!

Here is another interest-building routine that will help you become more attractive. If you have ever wondered how to guess the girl's age, here is your solution (assuming she asks first):

> **Her:** How old are you?
> **You:** Hmmm...it is more interesting to know how old you are. But do you believe in logic puzzles? Bet I can guess your age.
> **Her:** No way/Go ahead/ Really...(no matter what she says, you keep going.)
> **You:** Are you any good at simple math?
> **Her:** Yes/No, whatever...(if she says "No", let her get

her cell phone out and use the calculator. Tease her, please.)

You: Don't tell me how old you are, but add two to your age and then multiply it by three. Still with it so far?

Her: Yes.

You: Now, subtract six from the number you've got. Tell me the final result.

Her: 60. (Whatever number she tells you, divide that number by three in your thoughts, and you should get her exact age. It is simple math, and you have to be able to divide quickly. Let's say she is 18. (18+2)3 = 60, 60 – 6 = 54, 54/3 = 18. Got it?)

You: We all know that girls are sensitive about their age, so I want to make it fun and discreet. (Then whisper the number in her ears, don't say it out loud. Ask her to whisper back in your ears if you got it right. This is the important part of it and it should get the two of you closer to your common goal.)

Her: Wow, how did you get it?

Hope you liked it. It is simple and you can play with it. Plus after that she will ask you about your age again. You are sharing common information, building attraction and raising your self-esteem.

Those are only two of the many examples of tests that you can do. There are so many more out there. Why don't you go out there and find few more tests? Select the best ones you see, and modify them to match your style.

Remember, try to be interesting and creative in a positive way, not a needy creeper. Use these with a girl who's already shown some signs of interest, and don't pull them on girls who look too bored or annoyed. Be a gentleman!

Short Stories

Storytelling is something we will focus on another chapter, as you will need to be good at it once you start going on dates. The short stories that I speak about here are mostly used as interest builders. Here are some examples that you can use. If you don't have a personal story like that, make one up. Examples for easy hits:

- ✓ Tell her about a girl you know that cheated on her boyfriend and got caught.
- ✓ Share something you just saw happening in the bar ten minutes ago.
- ✓ Talk about your friend who became famous on social media by doing something cool.
- ✓ Say you have a girl friend that is like a sister to you. Tell her a story about her.
- ✓ Ask one of your buddies or a wingman to come over and tell a funny story you guys have shared.
- ✓ Ask a girl from your group to come over and tell everyone how you met, and how funny it was.
- ✓ Tell her about a music instrument you are playing, or a sport you do, or about another cool thing you do.

Short stories will give you an opportunity to show yourself in a different light that what she sees you in right now. They also provide plenty of opportunities for teasing, flirting, and building attraction. Be brief, as you don't want to get boring. Laugh a lot, and make your audience laugh.

Role Playing

My personal opinion is that role playing is a hard game to play. You have to be consistent, creative, and act a bit like a child. Remember when we were kids playing on the street the game of mommy and daddy? Now we are all supposed to be mature, and if not executed properly, the role play can give you a pretty bad reputation – that of a lame, childish, immature person.

Nevertheless, it is so much fun, and if you are good at it, everyone around you will enjoy it too. You need to be a great actor, and to be so confident that people will fall for your dramatic skills.

I do role playing exclusively to WRONG ONE type of girls (remember the types I mentioned in earlier chapters?). I love doing it with that type, because she tends to resist her attraction towards me in order to gain control. I like to flip a coin and play the game. Here are some of the roleplaying games I often do:

1. The relationship type "soap opera". I pretend she is my wife or my girlfriend. I act as if we have this hardcore relationship that is so full of drama that everyone knows about it – soap opera style. Have no clue what I'm talking about? Turn the TV on during the day and find a soap opera channel; then watch for few hours (if you manage to survive). Then you will get the point, I guarantee you. Drama is what we are shooting for here. Add a dash of humour, and you get a romantic comedy.

I'd say things like this, and then escalate them, to make it fun:

- ✓ Oh, honey, our relationship is going down. Your attitude is unacceptable.
- ✓ Darling, you take the kids, and I'll take the house and the car.
- ✓ Baby, our sex life is terrible. You always complain your head hurts, we need to have sex more often.
- ✓ I think you are cheating on me. Maybe with that guy over there...(point to the creepiest-looking guy in the venue).
- ✓ Honey, I'm cheating on you with an eighteen-year-old hot bikini model...

✓ Again, if lost, just watch an episode of any soap opera, take notes of the phrases, and use them. It's funny in an attractive way. It also shows tremendous amount of self-confidence.

2. The brother-sister story. OMG, girls respond in a funny way when faced with that role play. You act like their protective brother. This implies that you refuse to be attracted to them, which then makes them attracted to you. By doing this, you also communicate that you are not above her, but an equal, a brother-protector. After all, you are not really her brother. I'd say things like:

✓ Hey guys, this is my little sister, so behave. You are in big trouble if you hurt her feelings.
✓ Hey guys, this is my older sister. She is a bit grumpy and looks mean, but she's actually really nice inside.
✓ Hands off my sister! She is very sensitive, cute, and nice.
✓ Little sister, you are always so good to me I love you so much. (Followed by a kiss on the forehead.)

Now, remember that, if you once start, don't finish until reaching your goal, whatever that goal is. Also, do not overdo it, as it gets boring and annoying.

Space it out, or only make those comments when you actually want to spark interest or to tease her. Instead of blowing her off, tell her one of your phrases. Always do it in a group setting so you can get the reactions of the other people. Some might even join in the movie/soap opera.

Some other successful role playing games include: a job interview, general-soldier, boss-secretary, and patient-nurse.

Surprisingly enough, those are some of the most common role playing games husband and wives play during their night time adventures.

Coincidence? Not at all. Subconsciously, through your voice, intonation, and content, you might even unlock some of those sexual fantasies. Always be subtle. Role plating is fun for everybody, attracts attention, and bystanders are wondering if any of that is true.

Also check out tabletop roleplaying games. It's a great way to practice talking to other people and being a goofball, and can give someone a chance to play a hero. Also, a lot of gaming cafes and hobby stores have an open play night, and while many people there might already have significant others, they also often know single people. And a surprising number of cute, fun girls are gamers and tabletop role players. Plus, frankly, everyone is there to have fun and it's a good opportunity to loosen up and try something new.

The One Thing Few Men Do

A key point in to learn about the key interest women have – drama, fashion, emotions, personal relationships, etc. Educate yourself on those topics, be knowledgeable, and see how they look at you differently. Most women these days seem to read the news, and be active in talking about that stuff. Even if it's reality TV, women like to talk, think, analyse, and it's very, very rare to meet a woman who doesn't have an active social mind. Rather, she may be shy, or assume that nails and hair stuff won't interest men.

Remember, the single best thing a man can do, and perhaps the pinnacle of dating advice I can offer, is to not let 'boredom' stop him.

Even if you don't care about nail wraps or makeup, encourage her to talk about them and try to actively listen. Ask questions and tell yourself it's interesting. At worst, you'll learn stuff about something she loves. At best, genuine interest will make her feel like the most special girl in the room.

My Advice After This Chapter

Please go back and read this chapter again. Building interest, maintaining it, identifying if the girl likes you, and pulling some cool and interesting techniques, while presenting a challenge, is an ART. To be good at arts, you must be able to handle these two simple tools – creativity and practice.

"By recollecting the pleasures I have had formerly, I renew them, I enjoy them a second time, while I laugh at the remembrance of troubles now past, and which I no longer feel." — Giacomo Casanova

Please go back and read this chapter again! You will thank me later!

CHAPTER 14

Exciting Dating 101

As we already know, after mutual attraction is established, you have to move to the actual dating. While dating, your goal is just to be yourself, share stories, make her feel like you are compatible, and just be a cool guy, throwing out interesting jokes and stories all the time. Keep being challenging, and tease her, but not too much.

You want to be interesting, not annoying. You want to communicate confidently, but with certain sensitivity.

In this chapter, I will start with the controversial topic of flaking. Then I will follow up with my two personal favorite dating routines – the 3D and the Smooth Dating Routines. I have developed them when I was much younger, but they still seem to be 100% accurate. The basics are quite simple, so let's get to it.

Why Do Girls Flake?

I have been great at dating most of my life. It all came naturally to me. However, my pitfall was that I had a hard time learning how to take the girl out, if we go out. I'm interesting, challenging, and attractive, but the phone game and the flaking has been killing my dating life for a long time. Have you experienced the same?

"How can I show her how cool I am when I can't even take her out?" – I kept asking myself that question, until I found out few tricks to overcome it:

✓ You MUST start with accepting the fact that some girls will flake on you, and that it is completely normal. Refuse to have negative emotions if you get rejected. Keep this rarely known fact in mind! One of the biggest secrets with women is to never be too straight up and direct (as all of us usually are), and to never expect much, or make unrealistic plans. You've got to be creative and make dating look natural and unpredicted. Emotions are not allowed if flaked on, specifically ANGER. Getting pissed at girls flaking, or acting weird, will not help you at all.

✓ Always finish with a high point when sending texts or other online messages (Facebook, Twitter, Instagram, etc.). Let her send the last one and don't reply to it. If possible, stay away from the phone game, as it is very unpredictable and girls like to screw around.

✓ The worst part is that the best way not to be flaked on is to be flaky yourself. Remember do not overdo the flaking thing. Girls will tolerate you flaking, but will not tolerate you not doing what you said. In case you want to try how it works, just call her two hours in advance and say something else happened. By the way, texting is way better than a phone call.

✓ The Smooth Dating Routine is a great way to reduce the chance of getting flaked on. It also gives you a better chance of getting more dates, being creative, and not coming off as needy or desperate. You will seem like you have an interesting and dynamic life, and you want her to join you, while enjoying it. I will discuss the specifics of this routine in the next pages.

Let's be honest; girls fake and flake it all the time. Why are we trying to stay logical and punctual? Women live in their own emotional world, and we have to trigger their emotions rather than trying to be straight, direct, and logical. Be sensitive, please.

3D Routine

A few days before I wrote this chapter, I spoke with a friend of mine. He told me about this routine that I somehow managed to forget. He reminded me about an old strategy that I used back in high school. I still remember how I once shared it with him. It was years ago, and now the kid has a serious girlfriend that he got based on that technique. So I got pumped and wrote down this chapter.

For those of you that have a vibrant social circle, this strategy will be a deal maker. It is very simple, it works, and it is very, very quick.

I'd call it 3 Dates (3D), and guess why? You will only need three dates to make things happen. Nevertheless, before we go in detail about the specifics, we need to answer a simple question. How much time does it take between first meeting a girl and getting her as your girlfriend?

I would say about seven hours. You will read a lot of books on this concept, and most relationship authors out there will agree with me. I have noticed that I have so many interest-building techniques, stories, and things to talk about, but at around the seventh hour I do get bored. The girl gets bored too if nothing happens. Remember those seven hours; they will be your benchmark while dating.

Master the Art of the 3D Routine

I'm assuming at this point you have gotten a girl's contacts, and she shows you interest to the point where you can invite her for a date. Remember, going on way too many dates will diminish your chances for success. Girls like things to move smoothly, and they despise dating when it's either too rushed, or too slow. They also like variety.

Think about a girl you dated, yes, that one that you took on twenty-five dates and nothing happened?

Or think about the one you took on few dates, but of the same type – five walks in the park, or three times at the movies, or ten times for coffee. Boooooooooriiiiiiiing!

Variety is the key to keeping it interesting and different each time. So how do you spend less time dating, and get better results, while doing different things? Here is how you can do so.

Date 1: The Regular Date

You get the girl to come with you somewhere – a movie, a coffee, a walk in the park. Just spend some time with her. This is time for you two only.

Here are the key points:

✓ This is your one-on-one time. Be interesting and make sure you make her laugh.
✓ Take her to places no one else thought of, and be creative when it comes to selecting dating venues.

✓ Give her a NECKLACE, a RING or SOME OTHER PROP that you use. Tell her it is for luck and she can give it back to you next time she sees you.

✓ Always be the one to end the date. You are a busy guy; I'm pretty sure you have more things to do. Walk her home, and be a gentleman.

✓ I will spend more time in next chapters on how to get a great one-on-one date.

Date 2: The Date with Friends

Then you get her on another date, but she gets to meet your friends (social circle). If you are going out to the park with your buddies, to the beach, or for coffee, take her with you.

Here are the key points:

✓ Your buddies should tell great stories about you. They should support you. If somehow they lower your value, let them know. They should be helping not putting you down.

✓ Make sure you only bring out interesting, positive and social friends. You want her to see you surrounded by great people, as she will making assumptions about you based on your social circle.

✓ Make sure the group of people is mixed – girls and guys. If you take her out with your guy friends, it will be odd, and even dangerous. She might fall for one of them.

✓ If you have a female friend, a sister, or a female cousin, definitely bring them in. They can give you hugs, tell great stories about you, and most of all, this gives you a great opportunity to introduce some soft jealousy plots.

✓ Choose something fun, or a venue you can all enjoy. Choose something social – rollerblading, camping, dance classes, hiking, etcetera.

✓ Get your necklace from the previous date back (she'll give it to you). After the dinner, send her home with a kiss on the forehead, and hold hands.

Date 3: The Party Date

Take her out either clubbing or to a party. Then you can always dance with her, and get to be more intimate. By that time, she will be expecting you to move on. Stay confident!

Here are the key points:

✓ After the first two dates, the girl should feel much more comfortable with you. She should have built enough comfort with you, so you have to get going. Figure something out.
✓ Take her to a concert, to a club, to a bar, to a party of your friend, to your own party, to a picnic... somewhere social with your FRIENDS in your FIELD.
✓ Parties are a great place to get the positive vibe going. You can drink, you can dance, and you can have a lot of fun. No, you should definitely have a lot of fun.
✓ Bring in the shots. Say a lot of "cheers". Make sure you do not get way too drunk. This is not cool, and it does not work in your favor. Few drinks here and there, to get the mood flowing is OK. Going overboard is not.
✓ Here, you have to be the coolest guy – the one who gets the most attention, the real gentleman, the macho, the alpha male. Buy drinks at the club, dance a lot, and tell jokes. WIN THE CROWD.
✓ If you are at a club or at a party, your chances to kiss her are ten times better than if you go for a coffee, or for a walk at the park. The key to being successful at that date is to only go for the kiss. If she really wants sex, and is VERBAL about it (speaks openly about what she wants) then go for it, but otherwise, NO MORE THAN A KISS!

✓ Parties always provide more opportunities for you two to hide away from the crowd. Don't underestimate that.

The point of this technique is that she sees you from three different perspectives: as one-on-one person, as a friend, and as a party animal. Somehow, if you follow this strategy, your chances of getting a girlfriend are much higher. I know a lot of people that used this technique, and it did bring them success in dating.

At the end of the day, you want to have a successful dating routine that will power charge your lifestyle. You want to be able to write your own ticket to dating success, and to get the lifestyle everyone would be proud of.

The Smooth Dating Routine is Finally Here

Here is something interesting I figured out after I finished few dating books, and spoke with many friends on this topic. The purpose of the Smooth Dating Routine is to take the girl out without added pressure, while building comfort extremely fast. Women need to feel like things happen naturally.

A true gentleman knows the art of proper dating. Think about James Bond or any other fictional character, and how easily they make things happen. I can bet you right now, you'd love to know how they do it.

1. Innocent Activity (Hook).

I call it this because you invite the girl to do something simple and regular; it is friendly, and non-needy. You select regular activities that you have to do anyway. When you have those lined up, make sure you use that time and invite a girl to come join you. Your Saturdays or Sundays are perfect time for that.

You simply invite her to come help you with something or to see something else with you. You MUST set the date no later than 2 p.m. Choose early time of the day, because it is care-free for her. It will get her attention away from all those dinner and drinks based dates she is going to. Oh, yes, she is going to those, and she is looking for something different. After all, you want her to go out with you openly, not with all here defenses up.

Examples are:
- ✓ I'd like to buy myself a suit/belt/shoes/spring clothes. I need a woman's opinion. Do you want to come help me?
- ✓ I'm going to get my ears pierced. Would you like to come?
- ✓ I want to check this exhibition out quickly. Would you like to come see it with me?

What happens when you can't think of something real? What if you don't have to buy shoes, or get your ears pierced, or go buy birthday present for your friend?

Well, then you fake it till you make it. Say, "Let's go buy some shoes", then when you show up, say – "I'm going to buy some shirts on Saturday, and I'll buy shoes then too. I am going shopping for few things at the same time, it is better than just going five times."

MAKE SURE YOU TAKE HER HOME QUICKLY. TELL HER YOU FORGOT SOMETHING OR YOU HAVE TO DROP SOMETHING. TAKE HER HOME TO MAKE HER FAMILIAR AND THEN QUICKLY GET OUT. DO NOT STAY IN ANY LONGER. FOLLOW UPWITH YOUR SELECTED INNOCENT ACTIVITY.

Then take her out for a walk or coffee or whatever. If you don't have a set date, then make up one. Give your best to ensure it is not something every other guy will do. Again, be creative.

Also, try to get a friend of yours to come with you for the innocent activity and then leave all of a sudden. Man, it will be perfect. It looks natural, but it's actually pre-selected by you. It is also completely under your control.

2. The Bounce.

After you do your initial activity, take her for a coffee, lunch, or ice cream (preferred). Maybe before you are done with the first activity you can stop and grab something to eat. You've got to bounce her, as this builds both attraction and comfort.

Then use your interest-building routines: tell stories, use jealousy plots, role playing, make jokes etc. If you manage to bounce the girl to different locations, including your home on the same date, you will build so much more comfort that otherwise. It will take you several dates to just get talking.

3. Take me home

Offer to go back to your place for few drinks. She might experience enough comfort to say yes. This way, you took her for something regular and innocent, so her defenses were down. Then she liked you more, so she said YES to the bounce for coffee (instead of inviting her directly for coffee, which raises her defenses).

Then you were cool at the coffee, and this got her interested in coming to your place later on. Having a great night for both of you depends on how well you go from there.

A Note on the Regular/Trivial Dates

Being creative in a positive way will surely give you an advantage over other guys. I also wanted to touch on two very common dates – movie and coffee dates. We can't be always creative, and sometimes even the trivial and standard date might work. In case you wanted to know how to get those two dates right, here are my suggestions. Remember, always be smooth.

THE MOVIE DATE (a theater play works fine as well)

Goal: Break the Ice, nothing more

- ✓ Go online and see when the best cinema in town is playing a movie you want see. NO LOVE MOVIES, HORROR MOVIES, or MILITARY MOVIES. See a nice thriller, a funny comedy, or a good documentary.
- ✓ You can start by calling the girl two days in advance, and just chat with her for five minutes. Keep it simple. Then ask her if she wants to see a movie with you on a selected day. If she says yes, then tell her you'll call later on to tell her the details.
- ✓ Then call her later, tell her the details, and buy two tickets for the selected date and time.
- ✓ Then meet up with her see the movie. Do not attempt a kiss. Act as if she is your best buddy, but try holding hands at least for a while. Tell her she is fun and you should be FRIENDS, and go for a quick walk. Hold hands. Then send her home, give her a big HUG and a strong KISS on her CHEEK.
- ✓ NICE! You will manage to break the ice, and you won't feel like you have lost much energy, time or money.

THE COFEE DATE (Bubble tea works too)

Goal: Just chill, talk learn about her, nothing more

- ✓ You give her a COMFORT DATE. You can call her and invite her for a coffee. But you do ask her to be real and natural. No makeup, no fancy clothes.
- ✓ You want to see her real self, the way she looks every day. The best way is to go for a coffee somewhere near her home. This way she will feel safer and show up looking like a normal girl.
- ✓ Now, here is the key: be cool, show up with no gel on your hair, somehow sloppy-elegant. Smile a lot, and prepare some fun interest-building routines, jokes, and real life stories. I will give you more examples of thing you want to talk about in the upcoming chapters.
- ✓ Hold hands, and go for a quick walk. Send her home, but kiss both her cheeks and then her forehead. This will be confusing enough, but attractive at the same time.

My Advice After This Chapter

I will finish this chapter with one of my favorite quotes, something that you should keep reminding yourself:
GOOD MANNERS NEVER GO OUT OF STYLE!

Do yourself a favor, and try your best. Be funny, but respectful, confident, but not arrogant, chivalrous but not sleazy, persistent, but not needy, and amusing, but not a clown. The key to your future success at dating is finding that sacred balance!

"I love a man with a great sense of humor and who is intelligent – a man who has a great smile. He has to make me laugh. I like a man who is very ambitious and driven and who has a good heart and makes me feel safe. I like a man who is very strong and independent and confident. That is very sexy, but at the same time, he's very kind to people."
— Nicole Scherzinger

VANE CARNERO

CHAPTER 15

How to Have a Fantastic Conversation Without Breaking a Sweat

"The interesting thing is how one guy, through living out his own fantasies, is living out the fantasies of so many other people". — *Hugh Hefner*

We all know how to talk to other people, but not many of us know how to be an effective communicator. In order to be an interesting date, you need to be able to go out of your own frame, and go into the frame of the person you are dating.

What do they like, what do they hate, what gives them energy? You need things to talk about. I will go into detail about those questions in the next chapter. Before we do that, we will need to set some ground rules for proper communication.

✓ **Be a gentleman. Be Kind.** A true gentleman uses non-offensive language, he is respectful, he is sensitive, and most of all, he is clever. Don't be afraid to use street language, but do not sound like you just came out of jail. Respect the other person's views and values. A lot of guys love hearing their own voice, and they tend to interrupt other people. This is not cool, and if you are one of them, you should stop doing it.

✓ **Do not argue! Do not argue! Do not argue!** Should I say it one more time? I have so many friends who just love the thrill of arguing. And that is completely normal, as some of us like talking, and engaging in arguments with other people. Some of us learn this way. Some of us just love to debate. I am a great example of that. I like the idea of defending my point of view in a verbal communication. And because of that, I had a huge problem while dating.

My love for arguing made me do it on dates, too. Nevertheless, I managed to overcome it because I realised how pathetic I looked in those girls' eyes. Believe me, there is no bigger turn-off than a guy who is full of himself. Arguing is the biggest killer of attraction, and I can guarantee you, you will lose a lot of great girls because you can't restrain yourself. Be smart. Stop arguing, no matter how right you are. It will not work in your favour.

✓ **Adapt to their speaking style.** Have you noticed how some people manage to talk to anyone without any signs of pressure? One of the secrets to an effective communication is to adapt to the talking style of the person you are talking to. If they speak slowly, you speak slowly. If they speak quietly, you lover your voice. If they are loud, you raise your voice. If they move a lot while talking, you mirror their energy. You get my point. Adaptation is key here.

✓**Listen more, talk less.** A master communicator knows how important listening is. We have two ears and only one mouth, then why do we talk so much, and listen so little? Always ask yourself that question before you go out on a date. It will help you remember to ask the right questions, and to invest your dating time listening more than talking. Lie back on the bench in the park, ask a question, and just listen.

✓**Be a great storyteller.** Yes, I know I just told you not to talk too much. But again, when the opportunity presents, you should be able to take the remote control and tell some great stories. We all have so much to share, so many different experiences.

Keep in mind, the story you are telling has to be interesting, has to be entertaining, and has to be told in a way that it communicates a certain set of emotions. What's wrong with - "I just watched this movie, but it was way too long, and it was boring!"? It is way to factual. Guys love talking about facts, and their communication style with other guys is just like that – to the point, straight and simple.

Women, on the other hand, like to talk about emotions, and they love stretching the facts and covering their sentences in much more unnecessary words that what we usually do. Learn to stretch your sentences out, and make them more interesting to hear. To come back to the same example, you might want to try, "I just watched this movie, but I'm unsure about it… what are they trying to tell us? Have you seen it? Did you find it too long?"

✓**Keep an eye contact at least 70% of the time.** Keeping eye contact shows confidence. A lot of guys out there can't keep decent eye contact, which is sabotaging their dates. However, giving her 100% eye contact shows that you are too much into her. It comes off as quite needy and desperate, and can be creepy.

You want to keep a challenging personality, but not be way too hard to get. Remember to constantly look away from her for a few seconds. This is your tease technique. Look at someone passing by, and make a positive comment about something they are wearing. Then go back to the conversation.

✓ **Be careful of your body language.** Make sure you don't lean in too much, as it shows way too much interest. My practice has shown that acting as if you are at home works best. Let's say you went for a coffee. Sit back and enjoy it. Take that extra space by spreading your arms, keeping your distance, and act like you own the place.

Mix it up. Spend some time facing her while you talk, then face in another direction, but keep talking. Break the eye contact as you change your body position. Adopting a relaxed body language style is always very beneficial while dating.

✓ **Learn from other great communicators.** I have noticed that my friends that have some sales experience tend to be really good at it. Somehow, they have learned when to talk and when to listen, when to ask questions, and when to tell a great story.

If you have a friend who is heavily involved in sales, please do me a favour and go out few times with them over the course of the next weeks. Try to observe how they talk, how they listen, how they always lead the conversation. It feels like they are always in control. Being a great communicator is critical to your success in the dating world.

✓ **Please do not talk about your ex.** Doesn't matter how relevant it might be. Just don't do it at all. Like, don't lie and omit them from your life, but other than "I had a partner/spouse and now I don't," it's a guarantee that the person you're dating doesn't care and doesn't want to know. Likewise, if someone else breaks this rule, it's probably a bad sign.

Learn to listen actively, and lead by asking the right questions. Try to adapt to the speaking style of your date, do not interrupt, and restrain yourself from arguing. If you get a chance to tell a great story, please do so in an entertaining and attractive way. Don't just barf details at her.

Communicating in an attractive way is practice, not rocket science. The better you get at dating and the more you unlock your inner gentleman, the easier it will get to have a fantastic conversation with interesting women. Look at the next chapter for some great, field-tested sample questions that can elevate your conversation skills.

The Dating Questionnaire That Will Save Your Ass

People often ask me what they should talk about when they start dating a girl. In the end, it all comes down to simple psychology and social dynamics. Guys love talking about cars, money and sports. On the other hand, women love talking about emotions, relationships, and DRAMA. I have also observed that women love talking much more than men do. It is their way to vent from the negative experiences throughout the day. They do it by talking to someone about it. Have you noticed? Being a great listener is also very important.

This is my personal questionnaire developed to build comfort. The questions are grouped in different categories so you can checkmark them once answered. Remember, each question requires you to be able to follow up on the topic, and to be able to have a normal and interesting conversation about it. Be ready for her to ask you the same question in return. Prepare, prepare, prepare.

Personality Questions - Your Keys to a Great Conversation

Learning about her personality will not only be fun, but will tell you a lot about what you should expect in future dates, or from a possible relationship. Men love to talk about themselves, girls more so. You need to be gentleman about it, and use a smooth approach, but in the end, it is all about them talking a lot, and you acting like you enjoy it. Sometimes, you will actually enjoy it, believe me. It is fun learning about people.

✓ What is your star sign? – This is your chance to shine and show your astrology knowledge. Girls love that stuff. They love to talk about their personality traits, they love the tests, and they love anything that tells them something about who they are within. They will admire you if you know more on the topic. Do your homework before asking that question. I can personally talk for hours just on this topic. It is amazing, the kind of positive response you might get.

✓ Are you flaky or the serious type of a girl? – This is a great question to ask when you have just met, or on the first date, but not after. You will be able to set the rules on that topic, and share your perspective with her. She will share your thoughts and feelings, believe me.

✓ Extrovert or introvert? – Learn about the two personality types; there is so much info out there on the topic. You should be able to know which one she is without even asking. But asking about it shows you have interesting things to talk about.

✓ What is your favourite color? – There has been so much research on this topic. There are so many tests out there which will claim to tell you "your personality type based on your favourite color". Do your research.

✓ What is your favourite fruit? – You ask this question on the first date. Then, on the second one, you can accidently buy some. She will appreciate that you remembered. Think about the moment you take her home. How will she react if she sees a platter of her favourite fruits on the table? Be smart about it.

✓ Do you like to travel? – One of my favourite questions, because I can tell so many stories about my trips all around the world. It opens up the opportunity for you to show her how adventurous you are. You might also be surprised by how adventurous she is. Who knows?

✓ Do you like sports? – Again, if you do sports, you can easily talk about it. Hold on, what do I mean by "if you do sports"? You are watching your physique and your health, right?

✓ Are you spontaneous? – Great question. If she says yes, then she will love when you bounce between activities during your date, as I suggested in previous chapters. If she says no, then it is a great opportunity to tease her for being too normal.

What Does She Like About Dating?

Passion and relationships are the two most interesting topics a girl wishes to discuss. How would you feel if on the first date with a girl, she talked about cars, sports, winning, and succeeding in business? And what if she can really relate to those topics? I bet you would be all over her. She will be all over you if you know more about passion and relationships. The best way to convey your knowledge/expertise is to start a conversation with a simple question.

✓ What do you like in a guy's looks, behavior, and attitude? – This is a great conversation starter. Conversations on this topic can easily go for up to an hour if you really want to dig into it. It is a great way to see her values, beliefs, and to also identify a lot of her attraction switches. Ask this question on the first date, and you will thank me later on when you flip those switches like a pro.

✓ What do you dislike in a guy's looks, behavior, and attitude? – Same as above. You need to know the big NO's, as if you want a relationship, you will need to live with them. A note of caution – do not get emotional about her answers, and if you do not meet any of the expectations she mentions. Your goal is to talk about it, and to find ways to use the information she gives you to make yourself more desirable.

✓ How do you fall in love: fast, slow, or one step at a time? – You have to be very confident when you drop this one. Be ready to answer the same question after she gives you a very brief answer. You don't need to dwell too much on this topic, but it will surely create a spark.

✓ Are you in total control of your emotions? What do you know about emotional intelligence? – Ask yourself that same question right now. Do you personally know what emotional intelligence is? If you have no idea what it is, here is a great opportunity for you to check it out online. Maybe buy a book on it and educate yourself. The concept here is the same as the one in the Astrology question – knowledge is power.

✓ Is kissing cheating? Where is the cheating line? – This one will spark quite a long and emotional conversation. Always try to learn about her point of view.

✓ What do you want to do you never did so far?

It Might Also be a Great Idea to Learn About Her Social Circle

Know her friends: know what she likes in them, know what she doesn't like, know her family, and know what to expect when you meet them one day. Who you hang out with says a lot more about your personality than you could imagine. Have you noticed that your social circle is responsible, to a large extent, for your behaviour at the moment?

Your friends and family can influence how you act, how you think, and what you believe in, as you often share similar values and perceptions about the world. Knowing who they are and how they act will tell you a lot about the girl you are dating.

Here are some questions that you may ask:

✓ Are you a loyal friend? – A bit of a teasing question. It does not state it outright, but it implies that she might not be a good friend. Let her chase you on this one, and even if she says yes, let her justify it in a playful way.

✓ How many REAL friends do you have? Not the ones that hang around you just for company, the REAL ones? – This question opens up the topic, "how important is it for us to have real friends, not fake ones?" I've had a lot of great conversations using this question.

✓ Who is your best friend? – This gives you an opportunity to learn if there is a potential cockblock. What if her best friend is a guy? Get to know more here.

✓ Have you ever betrayed a friend? – A deeper and more unexpected question. Stir those emotions up. Create a "how loyal are you" role play. Be cheerful, teasing, and challenging in a fun way.

✓ Have you ever been betrayed by a friend? How does it feel? – Reach in for deeper emotions. Let's face it, everyone on this planet, guy or a girl, has been betrayed by someone they considered a friend. Didn't we all go through this? Yes, we did. So did she. So did you. This is a great opportunity for two of you to share some experiences from the past.

Learning about her family will get you one step closer if you are trying to get a serious relationship with this specific girl. If you are unsure of the desired outcome, then try to avoid talking about it unless she brings it up.

✓ Where are you from? Did you ever live in different locations?
✓ Who is the most influential member of your family?
✓ Do you have brothers/sisters?
✓ What is the best childhood moment?
✓ What is your worst childhood moment?
✓ What were you like as a kid?
✓ What kind of parent do you want to be?

I Would Not Advise You to Talk About Work While Dating

Work, career, money – topics NO girl likes to talk about on a date. It is boring to them, and most guys love talking about it. That makes it very, very risky. So how will you stand out, if you talk about something everyone else talks about?

Anyway, she might bring it up, so be prepared to answer quickly and ask in return. Make sure you do not dwell too much on those topics. You are not on a job interview! You can also tease her with that exact phrase if she brings up the topic of work and career.

✓ What do you do for living? Do you think this is what you were born to do? – Here is a creative way to turn a boring question around.

✓ What do you want to do in the future? What's your dream? – Again, turning an interview question into an emotional question.

✓ Where did you go to school? Did you party a lot? – It is all about turning a boring question into an interesting conversation.

My Advice After This Chapter

Remember that the abovementioned questions are not all of the questions out there that might work. You may have your own examples, so get a piece of paper and put down your own topics. Chose the ones that worked well in some of your successful dates.

Try to come up with at least five topics/questions. Then add the questions from this chapter (that you liked the most) to come up with a total of ten questions on your list. Put that list in your pocket every time you go on a date, and use it as a cheat sheet.

You may also create the list on your smartphone, but my practice has shown that stuff written on a hand works better for our subconscious mind. In case you run out of things to discuss and you start feeling awkward, or if the girl is too quiet, then excuse yourself, go to the bathroom, open your cheat sheet, and come back with more material to discuss. This routine did miracles for a lot of my friends. The list will save your ass in moments of confusion on lame and silent dates.

You can play around those basic questions and create unique conversation starters, interest-building routines, or even comfort boosters. Use these questions as a base and build upon them. This way you won't run out of topics to discuss.

Remember, as you practice more each day, you will become a much more confident version of your previous self.

CHAPTER 16

Why Some People Always Succeed at Relationships

"You know you're in love when you can't fall asleep because reality is finally better than your dreams." — Dr. Seuss

Having healthy and prosperous relationships is the final result of successful dating. Have you noticed that some people, who are outstanding at dating, truly suck at maintaining proper relationships?

The opposite is true as well. Some guys are so good when they are in a relationship, but they can't even approach new women when single. They are truly miserable when they have to go through the whole dating process. A smart and adaptable young man will have both types of friends. He will observe their behavior and will take notes.

Remember, to be good at dating requires you to have an attractive personality, to be open to meeting a lot of people, to be able to present a challenge, and to be good at starting a conversation. Being outstanding at relationships require another set of skills and behavior.

Being a happily married guy, I can definitely drop some hints about how you can make your relationships flourish. Yes, I know this book is about dating, but hey, we have to discuss what happens after you become very successful at it.

After all, we are in this for the ultimate goal – to be happily married, to have an amazing wife, and to be able to find your soulmate.

Getting successful at dating could have a very funny effect on some guys. Most of us, if not all, will end up in a relationship, but some of us will end up there even before they imagined or expected it.

After reading this, book some of you will end up in a relationship quite suddenly, and it will feel weird. Life will surprise you. I can tell you stories. Oh, yeah, I can definitely tell you stories...

A New Perspective that Will Get You Thinking

After reading a whole bunch of books on the subject of relationships and attending few dozen seminars, I managed to figure out something that changed my life forever.

All relationships can be summarized under three very simple categories – passionate, comfortable, and soulmate relationships. Let me tell you more about their differences.

1. Passionate Relationships

- ✓ They usually last maximum of two years, although they often last just a few weeks.
- ✓ You've all had those. They start so fast and end so quickly. There is so much drama.
- ✓ They are based on mutual attraction and passion, which often escalates too quickly.
- ✓ Sometimes we try to keep that relationship going even though we know there is no future in it.
- ✓ Your sex life is amazing. This is probably the only thing that works in that relationship.
- ✓ You constantly fight verbally. There are so many ups and downs, and you often engage in break up/make up activities.
- ✓ Your friends/family make fun of you being on and off all the time.

2. Comfortable Relationships

- ✓ They usually last twenty years. There is a normal/standard marriage at first, and then there is a divorce. People often get tired of dating, and they marry the wrong person for the wrong reason, and that reason is MUTUAL COMFORT.
- ✓ You both share financial goals, you are both well suited to raise a family, and you both want to have a family above all. People find their "better half", rather than their "other half".
- ✓ People usually settle for this type of relationship because it is easy. Your partner gives you all the resources, and has all the skills to raise a family with you.
- ✓ Often this relationship is boring, and partners feel like the reason is that they have settled. The truth is, they are completely wrong. The relationship fails because it is built upon being boring, standard, comfortable, and way too NORMAL.

✓ This relationship is based on mutual respect and dependence. Its primary goal is to raise children to be responsible adults. And guess what? That relationship is over exactly when kids are out of the home. The partners maintain the relationship "for the good of their children".

✓ Your sex life is boring and there is no "spark".

✓ You complete each other. You have some things in common, but you are so different in general. You often argue about your differences.

✓ A key here is that people often feel fear that they will not do well in life if they keep searching for their real soulmate, so they settle for the best second option. Congratulations! You have just lost twenty years of your life with someone for whom you have no passion.

3. Soulmate Relationships

✓ This is when you find a person that shares the same values, goals, passion, and looks as you. It happens when you pretty much meet your other half. You are partners and lovers at the same time. Your connection is inspiring for people around you.

✓ I know quite a number of couples that have achieved it, but they represent less than 5% of the relationships/marriages out there. Why? Because people settle for less.

✓ Both of you are interdependent, which means you both contribute significantly to the other one's well-being without being 100% dependent on one another. This is when either of you can succeed in life alone, but together, you triple your results.

✓ You work based on commonalities, rather than differences. You have very similar interests, taste, and hobbies. You often argue about your commonalities.

✓ When you go together at social gatherings, you are the one couple that stands out. You are often given as an example.

✓ You are both very passionate for each other, and your sex life is still thriving as the relationship progresses.

✓ You are both in a control of the relationship, and you share the leadership burden.

So, which relationship do you want to be in? Do you want to marry someone who will make your life boring, passionate, or both? Take a minute to think about it. There is no truly wrong answer.

Relationship Tips That Can Improve Your Lifestyle as a Couple

Let's get down to business. I've learned a few things about relationships, and I try to apply them every day. Here are some major tips for maintaining the relationship that I have developed over the years:

✓ Keep it **INTERESTING**. You must have an interesting and fun lifestyle that both of you enjoy. Love happens outside of home. Go travel, visit places, and experience new things each month. Simply do not forget to LIVE and be ADVENTUROUS, TOGETHER. Avoid getting too comfortable. Relationships are easily taken for granted, and people often ignore the importance of keeping it interesting.

✓ Keep it **CHALLENGING**. A woman will search the services of your neighbor as soon as your life gets simple and predictable. Remember it! Avoid being boring at all cost. DO NOT LET THE STABLE LIFE TAKE THE PASSION OUT OF YOU! If at some point of time you feel like you are stuck, or that things are going slowly, think about what you can improve.

✓ **CONTROL** your finances together. I know way too many couples where one of them is the "financial manager". This is ridiculously old school, in a bad way. We live in the twenty-first century. You should be both making money, and you should be both contributing to the family.

I've seen so many guys take care of this, so they automatically turned into the "daddy" type. Finances should be a shared responsibility, and you should both be in control. If you ask relationship specialists about the main reason relationships fail, they will name MONEY. If you think about it, it is not the money itself, but the way you both handle it that ruins everything. Be smart about it, please.

✓ **GROW** together. You must learn new things and evolve together as a couple, but also as individuals. Take the lead and make sure the growth is there in all three aspects: HEALTH, WEALTH, AND RELATIONSHIPS. Take courses together - learn a new dance, sport, or even a language.

✓ **SHARE** the responsibilities. You must delegate the duties. Do not take all the responsibility on your shoulders. The moment one of you takes more on their shoulders the balance is gone. This is not father-daughter relationship, where you will have to do all the work, provide all the guidance, and lead the way. It is not also the mother-son relationship, where you can't cook a decent meal, or wash your clothes.

Both of you need to know how to do everything at home. That is the first step. The second step is to assign a person to each task to balance things out. If one of you vacuums, then the other one throws out the garbage, or one cooks, the other does the dishes. If you don't set the rules early, you will both end up arguing about stupid shit like why the dirty dishes are still in the sink. Most families argue about basic, lame stuff all the time.

✓ Set **REMINDERS**. You must occasionally remind yourself of your PAST life, of what you want in the FUTURE and about how to make the PRESENT more fun. Say that three to four times a year, you will somehow analyze the relationship situation. Maybe at the beginning of each season, you pull out a piece of paper and white some goals.

Maybe on your birthday, Christmas, or New Year's Day, you remind yourself of it. Choose your own reminders. But don't forget them. Otherwise, fairly soon you will become the BORING family guy. You want to be the FUN family guy.

My Advice After this Chapter

I love relationships! They are AWESOME! Nevertheless, relationships can SUCK big time, especially for those dudes used to the single guy's lifestyle. It is particularly painful if you are accustomed to doing whatever you please.

Your girl will want to spend all her time with you, and if you don't, she will make your life miserable. If you are that type of a guy, you need to learn to co-exist with other people under the same roof. It will take a lot of devotion, patience, and learning on your behalf.

If you want to have a great soulmate relationship one day, make sure you have a lot of practice. Live with other people, and move in with your current girlfriend, because you will need that practice.

The best part of it is that HEAT Lifestyle can be equally applied for a single guy's life and for a couple in a relationship. You just have to keep the balance together. There is nothing better than enjoying a dynamic and interesting life with someone who loves you and shares your desire to appreciate life.

"At the end of the day, 'Rocky' is a love story, and he could never have reached the final bell without Adrian."
— *Sylvester Stallone*

VANE CARNERO

THAT'S IT!

Do the Homework, Change Your Life

When I was looking for an editor for this book, I stumbled upon a very nice lady with a lot of editing experience and a total lack of appreciation as to what this book is. According to her, the majority of book readers are women in the age group 35-50. She also told me the males in the age group 18-40 do not read many books.

So why was I writing a book for guys, then? According to her, I should have dropped the topic, and chosen something else to write about.

Well, as I mentioned in the beginning of this book, the world is full of bad advice. I chose not to follow that advice, and here it is. There is someone finishing this book. Someone I'm really proud of. Whether a guy or a girl, eighteen or forty, you have finished it. That is all that matters to me. Fix yourself a drink and celebrate!

Now, go to that page at the beginning of the book where you wrote your goals and expectations. Did you meet them? Did you do your homework? Did you practice what you saw here?

I really hope you liked what you read, and I'm looking forward to hear your success stories. Find me online and hit me up if you have questions, comments, or concerns. I'm all over social media, and I love to talk to interesting people.

I hope you enjoyed this book just as much as I loved the journey that inspired me to write it. I also hope one day you could find your significant other (motivated by your knowledge gained while reading it). In the end, there is nothing better than enjoying a dynamic and interesting life with someone who loves you and shares your desire to appreciate life.

Good luck! Stay smooth, be smart, and act like a true gentleman!

Vane Carnero

BEYOND ATTRACTION

VANE CARNERO